How to get to the top of   Q

GOOGLE
SEARCH

A practical SEO guide

RANDOM HOUSE

UK | USA | Canada | Ireland | Australia
India | New Zealand | South Africa | China

Random House is an imprint of the Penguin Random House group of companies, whose
addresses can be found at global.penguinrandomhouse.com.

Penguin
Random House
New Zealand

First published by Penguin Random House New Zealand, 2019

1 3 5 7 9 10 8 6 4 2

Text © Richard Conway, 2019

Design and illustrations by Rachel Clark © Penguin Random House New Zealand
Prepress by Image Centre Group
Printed and bound in Australia by Griffin Press,
an Accredited ISO AS/NZS 14001 Environmental Management Systems Printer

A catalogue record for this book is available from the National Library of New Zealand.

ISBN 978-0-14-377353-5
eISBN 978-0-14-377354-2

penguin.co.nz

How to get to the top of   Q

GOOGLE SEARCH

A practical SEO guide

RICHARD CONWAY

SEARCH ENGINE SPECIALIST

RANDOM HOUSE
NEW ZEALAND

ACKNOWLEDGEMENTS

I would like to say a big thank you to all who helped with or contributed to this book: Rand Fishkin, Larry Kim, Georgi Todorov, Iyia Liu, James McGlinn, Jennifer Johnson, Cornelis Boertjens, Michael Speight, Linda Coles, Tony Mitchell and Oxford Lamoureaux. For the awesome work from the ladies at Intelligent Ink: specifically Christina Wedgwood and Briar Lawry. Dr Julia Fehrer from the University of Auckland and Patrick Dodd from Unitec. John Maloyd, Deon Metcalf and Uli Knapp for your support in the early days. Tony Falkenstein and Ian Malcolm for sharing the journey and believing in me. Dallas Rabot and Prabin Yonzon for your top-class SEO knowledge and technical input. The whole team at Pure SEO and my family: Emily, Ethan and Amber. Thank you all.

CONTENTS

PART ONE: ON-PAGE SEO

PART TWO: OFF-PAGE SEO

PREFACE

Can you remember your first experience with Google? For most of us, it's been a taken-for-granted part of our experience on the internet since the beginning of time (or at least since the beginning of the internet . . .).

However, I can remember my earliest significant interaction with it. It was the end of 2002, and I was working in-house at a commercial property fund in London, which up until that point had been spending about £180,000 a year advertising in *The Times*, the *Telegraph*, the *Independent* and other publications in order to get in front of buyers of commercial property. I set up my Google Ads campaign and reduced our advertising media spend to £25,000 the next year, while fielding double the enquiries. I couldn't help but think 'Hang on — there's something in this!'

Various roles in digital strategy and campaigns for some of the biggest companies and brands in the UK followed, and I've been involved in SEO (that's search engine optimisation) ever since. Although the field has changed and evolved a lot since then, I've seen the value of search engine marketing since those beginnings.

But how did I come to start New Zealand's largest specialist search agency? Well, about 15 years ago, also back in the early 2000s, my girlfriend at the time (now my wife) Emily and I set off travelling, exploring Australia, New Zealand and various parts of Asia. Although we returned back home to the UK, we left some of our hearts in New Zealand during that first trip.

We talked about moving, and knew that New Zealand would be an incredible place to have and raise kids, but the years (six, in fact!) ticked on. In the interim, we got married. But then, as we neared 30 and realised that if we didn't leave soon we probably wouldn't, we both resigned from great jobs, packed a few bags and got on a plane . . .

In 2009, we touched down in New Zealand. We knew no one, and quickly discovered how hard it was to find employment at a reasonable rate of pay because we didn't have the right Kiwi experience. I knew I had valuable skills and experience to offer, though.

I had always wanted to start a business, so off I went — in the field that I knew. When I looked around the New Zealand market, people were doing dodgy things and gaming Google's algorithms in different ways. Not only that, but the two main agencies that were doing SEO well at the time were focused on servicing corporates. I could see there was a gap for an ethical player, and one that was looking after small and medium-sized enterprises (SMEs) — especially given that it's these organisations which make up the majority of the New Zealand economy.

It was now or never and, in some ways, I had very little to lose: we were renting, Emily was working, and we didn't have kids yet (although we were trying). I was in a new country, and starting from nothing. But I started.

The name Pure SEO came from Emily and me just throwing things about; we were (and still are!) enamoured with 'Pure New Zealand' and I knew I wanted to be a specialist SEO agency, as opposed to all things digital marketing. Our logo was originally designed by a friend of ours, John Maloyd, for the total cost of a bottle of Grey Goose vodka. (John, you're a legend!) Our first website was one page that I paid a guy $200 to do, before I cobbled together the rest of the website. I'm embarrassed to say now, it looked like a child had done it.

Starting out, I had none of the things that might have made this journey easier: I had no established network in New Zealand, and the majority of the money we had was still tied up back home. We had come with only a little cash, and this was at a time when the pound was dropping in value, so there was no sense in bringing over the rest. But I did have the drive ... I remember getting up and sitting in my dressing gown in the living room of our rented apartment, wondering where on earth I was going to get business.

I read Richard Branson's book *Losing My Virginity*, which taught me that if you don't have the budget (and we certainly didn't), you need to raise your public profile in order to build a business. This helped me to make the decision to get out of my comfort zone and raise my profile from day one. I've never been comfortable with self-promotion — I'm traditionally a peripheral character and I don't like being 'front and centre' — but I went to events and started talking to people. I would show up and know nobody, then look for other people standing on their own, and strike up a conversation with them. I joined Business Network International (BNI) New Zealand and Business Mentors New Zealand, and soon my network was growing.

The business was growing, too. Getting our first client, Creative Embroidery, was a turning point. I kept moving forward, busily embracing what Kiwi entrepreneur Claudia Batten refers to as 'vomit moments'— pushing the boundaries, taking risks and doing things that were uncomfortable; that's a lot of what my entrepreneurial journey was about. I had hired our first employee long before I could afford them; same with the second. Thankfully, by the time our third hire came on board, we had enough recurring revenue each month to know that we could cover the bills — including the wages.

So, by our second year in business, it was no longer me in my dressing gown; we were up to four staff and we were doing it. I invested $10,000 on a new website, which seemed like a fortune to me then, and the first enquiry that came through it was from Singapore Airlines! It was a timely reminder of the incredible power and value of having that 'shopfront'; you can be pretty much whoever you want to be online. That year, I also signed insurance company AIA, who stayed with us for seven years. I remember pitching 'we' and 'us', when it was really just mostly me. Fake it till you make it . . .

On the personal front, we faced some challenges; Emily and I experienced three miscarriages that year, before she eventually fell pregnant with our son Ethan. Needless to say, it was a stressful and emotionally fraught time. I had to front up to work each day and play at being a leader. I was growing a business, and there were people expecting things from me; I had to be there, and deliver, as well as having these other difficulties going on. It was lonely and just plain hard some days.

It was around this time that, through BNI, I met Uli Knapp and Deon Metcalf, who owned a web development company. Not only was it a natural fit in terms of delivery, but they also had space in their office in Auckland's Viaduct. The opportunity to work away from my kitchen table was invaluable, and my first staff member perched on the end of my desk there. Uli and Deon even wanted me to tag along with them as they moved into a new space in Parnell; that invitation alone was incredibly fortuitous.

Thinking that I was a better negotiator than the two of them, Uli and Deon sent me in to liaise with the landlord regarding this new space . . . Enter Tony Falkenstein. Tony's business reputation preceded him, and I took the opportunity to ask him to grab a coffee with me and allow me to pick his brains. Fortunately he agreed, and I cannot overstate the impact that Tony has had on my life and business journey.

Tony introduced me to the world of EO (Entrepreneurs Organization), initially through their accelerator programme, Ignition, which I joined in 2012. I remember the first trip away that we did, down to Queenstown, where I really threw off the bow-lines — and threw myself out of a plane for my first-ever skydive, despite my fear of heights. That pretty much sums up how I thrust myself into this tight-knit business world: head-first. The learning was invaluable, but the social side was still difficult to begin with; I knew no one in the group.

As well as meeting some incredible other business people and entrepreneurs through both Ignition and EO, I was also introduced to Tony's accountant, Ian Malcolm, who soon became my accountant, too. Clearly he saw something he liked as, in 2014, Ian approached me about whether I would consider selling him a share of Pure SEO. Tony purchased 25 per cent of the business and Ian a further 10 per cent. This was one of the best decisions I ever made. Not only was I able to become mortgage free, I had also teamed up with really experienced business people who had an incentive — skin in the game — to help me in growing the business.

We should have been going from strength to strength at this point, and in some senses we were, but then there were personnel issues (our key staff member handed in their resignation). Our personal challenges weren't over, either . . . Following the discovery of a lump on her neck after a Sunday KickFit class, Emily was told she had thyroid cancer. To begin with, we didn't know what the outcome of this diagnosis would be, and I recall the inner turmoil I felt when I first had to call our family back in the UK.

Luckily Emily's diagnosis turned out not to be terminal. However, she had a total thyroidectomy and a lot of lymph nodes removed, and underwent radioactive iodine treatment therapy, following which she had to spend a week in total isolation in a lead-lined room in the hospital. Eventually she recovered, but it was a long and emotional road. Most of the care of Ethan, who was an energetic toddler at that point, fell to me, at the same time as I was still trying to run the business. Thankfully my parents flew over to help out, and we got through it. We weren't sure if we would be able to have any more children following Emily's ordeal, but fortunately our daughter Amber came along not too long later.

While these challenges may not be directly linked to Pure SEO's story, they're an inextricable part of mine. They also made me appreciate what I had, consider that we might only have today, and look at my priorities differently. I also think it's probably just as well I'm naturally wired to be an eternal optimist. My favourite quote is one by Winston Churchill, and it sums this disposition up well:

An optimist sees the opportunity in every difficulty.

A pessimist sees the difficulty in every opportunity.

To me, life is always about learning, and I've learnt a lot (and continue to do so) — from the reality that no one (literally no one, not even me) is indispensable, to the fact that good systems and processes make all the difference, and that transparency is key to building trust. I've learnt to accept that you can't please everyone, and to appreciate that everyone thinks differently, which led to the realisation that hiring a team of people who are better than you at certain things is essential to helping your business grow.

I've made mistakes, too — trying to do my own accounts to start with, keeping everything in my head instead of documenting anything for our first 50 clients, and over-promoting people or not getting rid of bad fits quickly enough. However, at the end of the day, I love what I do. I may not be a natural leader — I'm too soft, don't love detail and wear my heart on my sleeve — but I also try my best, unwaveringly, and lead by example.

We are now the largest specialist search agency in this part of the world. We're the most awarded, too. Anyone who has been through the process of entering business awards will understand about the time and work involved. This has been invaluable for our team, though, and has provided me with the opportunity to look back and appreciate where we've come from, rather than getting stuck in the daily grind.

Essentially, the business model that Pure SEO operates under now is the same one that Emily and I dreamed up over the kitchen table back in 2009. Back then, I created the following mantra, which still serves as our beacon — and the reason we exist — all these years later:

> At Pure SEO we believe in relationships that are based on trust. When we work together, we are going to do our best to serve you – going above and beyond and out of our way to do exactly what we say we are going to do. We will act in a manner that we would want and expect for ourselves, and follow an ethical path, always keeping honest and leading by example at every turn.

There are a lot of sharks in this industry, and we believe in being an ethical alternative. Not only that, but many of the other cornerstones of the business remain today, too — including our core values of trust, respect, integrity and family. It was our BHAG (big hairy audacious goal!) right from the start to get to number one on Google for SEO; in this business, if you don't rank, you don't know what you're doing. We achieved this within 18 months of launch, but, like any business, we have had to put in the work consistently to stay there.

I never thought that I would have more than 50 people relying on the business I created for their income. But this business is like a family, with a culture of its own. We believe that our diversity gives us strength — with 16 nationalities represented among our team and a 50:50 male:female ratio at a leadership level. We also believe in having fun.

Although we're the largest in our field, with 65 people in five offices across three countries, I can still picture exactly what we need to do next in order to keep growing. I believe that if you stay still, you're effectively going backwards, so I always have an eye on what's coming in order to stay ahead of the curve and lead the industry. We will continue to push boundaries and evolve our offering — we've recently launched a corporate product, and are looking to open two more offices in Australia.

It's been a wild ride — that guy just starting out in his dressing gown could not have imagined that he'd have the opportunity to spend a week with Richard Branson on Necker Island! From Uli and Deon, to Tony, and countless others who have been a part of this journey, I'm incredibly grateful for how many people have given so generously of their time and experience while expecting little in return; that's been massive for me! It's from a place of appreciation, as well as the foundation of our belief in truly helping New Zealand businesses, that this book has come.

I built this business using good digital marketing because it's cost-effective and it works. I have not only my own experience but so many of our clients' journeys that I've played a part in to share with you to help you do the same.

I firmly believe in giving freely of knowledge and edu-cating the market. As well as speaking engagements and teaching roles within the industry — including writing the NZQA SEO course for Unitec and lecturing for the University of Auckland MBA programme — it's important to me that even more people can access the information they need to effectively DIY their SEO. All of the information is out there, but this book compiles what you need to know, from an Australasian 'best practice' perspective, and in real speak. At the end of the day, I'm not a technician; I'm a marketer and a business person, and this book is from that perspective.

You hold in your hands the difference between ranking and not. I'm excited to be sharing with you the ability to truly impact your bottom line.

GLOSSARY

404 pages — an error message or standard HTTP response code that shows that a page wasn't able to be found. It means that the content you're trying to access isn't there, despite having a good internet connection and being able to communicate with the required server.

A/B testing — a test, or experiment, where two versions of a single variable are tested ('A' option and 'B' option), to see which gets a better response. The results are then compared in order to determine which variable or option is the more effective one.

above the fold — refers to the portions of a web page that are visible on a screen without scrolling or clicking. The term is derived from the upper half of the front page of a traditional newspaper, where the most important news story was published.

algorithm — a program or formula used by search engines that determines which pages to suggest in response to a specific search query. This is controlled by the search engine itself and is subject to changes as and when they choose.

alt attributes (alt tag, alt text) — words used to describe or explain an image. Useful for those who are visually impaired (in which case these are often read out loud by special browsers). When images don't display, alt attributes help a search engine tell one image from another. Alt attributes are an important thing to optimise (see chapter 2).

AMP (Accelerated Mobile Pages) — an open-source initiative by Google and Twitter that allows website owners to create super-fast-loading mobile web pages.

anchor text — the visible and clickable text of a hyperlink, which can be optimised far beyond the generic 'click here' or 'read more'. Anchor text helps to indicate the relevance of a site, and the content you're linking to, to search engines (see chapter 2).

AR (augmented reality) — technology that superimposes a computer-generated image on a user's view of the real world. See also VR.

authority — in search land, authority means the amount of trust or credibility (otherwise referred to as 'link juice') a site has as it relates to a particular search term or query. Authority mostly derives from incoming links (see chapter 12). As an example, the Penguin Random House website has lots of good-quality links coming into it — as opposed to Joe Bloggs the plumber who has only just started his business — which means that Penguin Random House would have greater authority.

'black hat' SEO — ethically questionable practices that aim to game or cheat the system and go against 'best practice' standards.

blog — a website or web page that is updated regularly with fresh content and new articles. New blog posts are typically added to existing content, as opposed to replacing what's there. They were originally intended to be written in a relatively informal and conversational style, although they now much more commonly reflect the tone of the individual company.

bot — see crawler.

bounce rate — the percentage of visitors who leave your website without viewing any of the other pages. In other words, they land on one page and then leave.

breadcrumbs — a website element designed to make navigation easy. It usually displays up the top of a website page and allows users to retrace their steps, much like in the fairy tale 'Hansel and Gretel'.

CMS (content management system) — a software application, or series of related programs, used to create, modify and manage digital content published on the internet. WordPress is the most popular CMS used on the web.

content creator — someone who creates content for use online, whether it be written content in the form of blogs, or videos or podcasts.

content curation — the gathering and culminating of other people's content related to a particular topic or area of interest, as opposed to writing something brand new.

content delivery network (CDN) — a system or network of distributed servers that can serve up web pages to a user based on their geographic location, the origin of the web page and the content delivery server used.

content marketing — a type of marketing that involves creating and sharing online content — whether it be in written blog format or as videos — that doesn't explicitly promote a brand or business, but is intended to indirectly increase interest.

conversion funnel — a term used in e-commerce to describe the journey a user takes through search or advertising, and around a website, before ultimately converting to a sale.

conversion rate — the rate at which people achieve the quantifiable goal of your site, whether that is signing up to something, making a purchase or filling out a form.

country code top-level domain (ccTLD) — a unique two-letter sequence that's assigned to each country or geographic area, allowing it to be identified in a domain name (e.g. nz or au).

crawler (also referred to as a bot or spider) — a program that moves through the world wide web, visiting websites and reading their information. Crawlers gather data and links to store in their databank for search engine indexing.

CRO (Conversion Rate Optimisation) — increasing the percentage of website visitors who convert into customers or complete the desired action on that page.

CSS (Cascading Style Sheet) — part of programming language used for describing the presentation of a web page written in a markup language, or code, like HTML. Basically, it describes how HTML elements are to be displayed on screen and can save a lot of work when you're laying out multiple web pages.

CTA (Call to Action) — a piece of content, usually in the form of an instruction or directive, intended to induce the user to perform a specific action, like 'Download our ebook now'.

CTR (Click-through Rate) — used to measure the effectiveness or success of an advertising campaign, click-through rate is the ratio of users who click on a specific link to the total number of users who view that page or advertisement. It's calculated using total clicks on ad or page divided by total impressions (or page views). A high CTR means that a high percentage of people who see your ad, listing, link or whatever you're measuring click on it and follow it through.

digital engagement — online methods of engaging with customers or potential customers.

domain authority — a search engine ranking score (out of 100), calculated based on factors such as number of links and integrity of the places they're coming from. It is used to predict how well a website will rank in search engine results.

dynamic design — a website design which sends an entirely new version to a mobile device, to be viewed perfectly on that device. For contrast, see responsive design.

EAT (Expertise, Authoritativeness, Trustworthiness) — an acronym that indicates the importance of high-quality website content. EAT is among the top three considerations by Google when it comes to judging the quality of web pages.

EDM (email direct marketing) — email-based campaigns or marketing communications that are sent directly to a targeted list of recipients.

Flash (or Flash plugins) — a multimedia technology developed in the mid-90s to allow web developers to incorporate animations and interactive content into websites.

fold — see above the fold.

follow/nofollow links — a follow link is one where the SEO benefit is passed from one website to another in the form of a clickable link (kind of like a vote for that website). A nofollow link is one where the link exists but does not pass on the SEO benefit (usually found on paid links, blog comments and social media, to stop people spamming them with links).

gamify — introducing game-like elements or principles in a non-game setting, usually in order to improve user engagement or participation.

Google Ads — Google's online paid advertising program, used to display short adverts, service offerings, product listings and video content within Google search results.

headers — the title of a post or emphasised text on a page. They are formatted using a header tag or <H1> in HTML.

hreflang tags — a component that specifies the language and optional geographic restrictions of a website, or what areas or languages it is targeting with its content.

HTML (Hypertext Markup Language) — a programming language that provides a standardised system for tagging web-page text to display various fonts, colours, graphic and hyperlink effects.

HTTP (Hypertext Transfer Protocol) — the underlying protocol or code that the internet uses to determine how information is formatted and transmitted, and how web servers should respond to various commands.

hyperlink — see link.

impression — a page view. An impression is counted every time your site is viewed.

inbound links (or back links) — a hyperlink on another website that points to a page on your website. Inbound links from related high-quality pages are a source of trust that helps your search engine ranking.

IoT (Internet of Things) — the interconnection of devices embedded into everyday objects, which can send and receive data over the internet.

JavaScript — a programming language commonly used to create interactive or dynamic effects on web pages. JavaScript code can be inserted anywhere within the HTML of a web page.

keyword — a word (or in some cases, phrase) that users enter into a search engine. These are the things you want to be known for or associated with. Keyword research will help you to determine which keywords are appropriate (and achievable) to target.

landing page — the page that a visitor to your site views first (lands on) when they click on a link in the search engine results. This should be the most relevant page to that search query — not always simply the homepage of your site.

link (or hyperlink) — an element of a web page, signalled by specially formatted text, that takes the user to another web page or another part of the page they are viewing.

link equity — the influence that a link has on a page's ability to rank in search engine results, based on authority, trust and relevance to the content of a page. Think of it as a credibility-bolstering scenario, as this is based on the idea that certain links pass value and authority (or a lack thereof) from one page to another.

link juice — a slang term denoting how powerful a particular link from a website is. The idea is that a link from a more trusted website (one with greater domain authority) will provide more 'juice' than one from a pointless directory.

long tail — a search query that is longer or more descriptive than a single keyword. A large percentage of search queries are long tail, as opposed to people typing in a single word.

Maps Pack — a boxed area at the top of the first Google search engine results page that displays the top three local business listings deemed most relevant to a search query. Also known as the Snack Pack, Local 3 Pack or Google 3 Pack.

metadata — information about a website that a search engine receives that visitors to your website don't see on the site, but see in the search engine results pages.

meta title (also referred to as a page title tag or title tag) — a bit of HTML code in the header of a web page that gives a brief description, designed to help search engines, and human searchers, understand the content of a web page.

mobile-first index — search results ranked by the mobile version of a website.

nofollow link — see follow/nofollow links.

off-page SEO — actions taking place outside of your actual website that affect your website's ranking in search engines, e.g. link building, social media and influencer marketing.

on-page SEO — anything that can be done directly within a website — either to the content or HTML code — in order to rank more highly and be found by relevant users accessing search engines.

organic search/traffic — visitors who come to your website as a result of your ranking on a search engine results page, as opposed to those who have clicked through from a paid advertisement. Organic search traffic is influenced and improved by effective SEO.

open-source — software for which the original source code has been made freely available. The software itself is also free and is open to be redistributed and modified.

page title tag — see meta title.

plugins — a software component that adds a specific feature to an existing computer program. These additions or extensions are generally easily installed and used within the original program that they are designed to enhance.

position zero — a snippet, implemented by Google, that displays in the top part of a search engine results page and gives a summary of the best result (as judged by Google) in response to a searcher's query.

PPC (pay per click) — also known as CPC or cost per click, it's an internet advertising cost model whereby the advertiser pays the publisher or host a fee each time their advertisement (which is set up to drive traffic to their website) is clicked.

rank — a website or web page's placement on a search engine results page. A high ranking means you are close to the top of the first page of results displayed. SEO strategies are geared towards helping websites to achieve a higher ranking.

reciprocal linking — a mutual hyperlink between two websites. When done well, it denotes a partnership, or indicates that the sites cover similar topics and provide further reading or services to each other. The practice is not viewed favourably by search engines if it doesn't really make any sense for the sites to link to each other.

responsive design — where a single website design automatically changes to fit the device it is viewed on (mobile, tablet, desktop). For contrast, see dynamic design.

robots.txt — a file in the background of a website that controls or restricts the behaviour of web crawlers or spiders.

ROI (return on investment) — the ratio between the profit or benefit of an activity compared to the cost of doing it. The benefit (or return) is divided by the cost of the investment, with the result given as a percentage or ratio.

search engine — a program that searches the world wide web to find content that relates most closely to a user's keywords, returning a list of the most relevant matches as a series of links. Google is, by far, the most used search engine in New Zealand and Australia.

SEO (search engine optimisation) — activities that optimise a website or web page to achieve the highest possible ranking on a search engine results page. The ultimate aim is to increase the quantity and quality of organic visitor traffic to a website or page. See also on- and off-page SEO.

SERP (search engine results page) — the pages displayed by a search engine in response to a query by a user. The main component may be listings of results in response to a keyword query, but these pages also include other results like advertisements.

spider — see crawler.

text to speech (TTS) — a form of speech synthesis that converts text into spoken-word output.

title tag — see meta title.

top level domain (TLD) — the last segment of a domain name (after the 'dot'). These are typically classified as either generic (e.g. '.com') or country-specific (e.g. '.co.nz').

traffic — the visitors who arrive at a website or web page. Traffic can be either paid (through the use of ads, etc) or organic (which results from people who land there as a result of your SEO efforts and unpaid, natural ranking within search engine results pages).

trust — in internet terms, think of links as 'votes' for a website. At a basic level, the more 'votes' you have, the more trust you have. However, not all votes are equal: a vote from somewhere like *The New Zealand Herald* or the University of Auckland would be worth much more than a vote from Joe Bloggs the plumber.

URL — a web address. URL stands for 'uniform resource locator' but it's rarely (if ever) used in this expanded form.

vlog — a blog on which the content is primarily posted in video format (video blog).

VR (virtual reality) — the computer-generated simulation of a three-dimensional image that can be interacted with in a seemingly real way via the use of special electronic equipment such as a helmet, visor or gloves. See also AR.

W3C (World Wide Web Consortium) — an international community that establishes the standards, guidelines and protocols for the world wide web.

WAYMO — a self-driving technology development company, originally started by Google before becoming a stand-alone subsidiary in December 2016.

INTRODUCTION:

A LOOK AT WHAT SEO IS – AND ISN'T!

Every month you don't invest in SEO is a month when
your competitors will, and eventually, even if you have
a long head-start, they'll catch up and surpass you.

– Rand Fishkin, founder of SparkToro, founder
(and former wizard!) at Moz.com and author

I couldn't agree more with this statement, and I suspect you've
got an inkling of this, too — unless you're still out there in the
trenches, getting surpassed by your competition. Good news:
this book will definitely help.

First, let's deal with the elephant in the room: 'SEO is dead.'
'Search marketing is old school.' People have been saying
this — and many other similar inanities — for ages. They will
probably continue to do so. We were recently the subject of a
rant by a disillusioned soul who was criticising us for having
signwritten cars and engaging in radio advertising, as though
that were evidence of the demise of digital/search marketing.

However, the fact that you're here — reading this book — shows that you know, as I know, that they're wrong. Utilising a range of marketing channels just makes good business sense (as you'll see in chapter 11, which looks at how to bring search together with your other marketing). I'm getting ahead of myself, though. The legitimacy and pervasiveness of search in its own right is fairly compelling proof.

Ask anyone if they've used Google in the last 24 hours and the answer is, unequivocally, yes. We're all doing Google searches, every day, to find products and services. And it's not just young people: I recently gave a talk at the Auckland City Rotary Club and asked that same question; almost everyone in the room put up their hand. This was an audience of people in their sixties, seventies and eighties, which to me shows just how endemic our use of search is.

According to website Internet World Stats, over 4.2 billion people worldwide use the internet. IWS also reports that Google now handles more than 1.2 *trillion* searches a year — which translates to more than 40,000 searches every second — and apparently this number is growing. In fact, web-traffic analysis tool StatCounter shows Google's month-by-month search impression share here in New Zealand sits at 95 per cent.

By comparison, in Australia Google has a 93 per cent search impression share.

Given that's where so many eyeballs are looking, the need for good search marketing is far from gone.

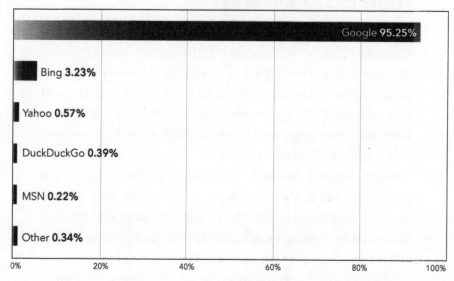

StatCounter global stats
Search engine market share New Zealand from Aug 2017 – Aug 2018

- Google **95.25%**
- Bing **3.23%**
- Yahoo **0.57%**
- DuckDuckGo **0.39%**
- MSN **0.22%**
- Other **0.34%**

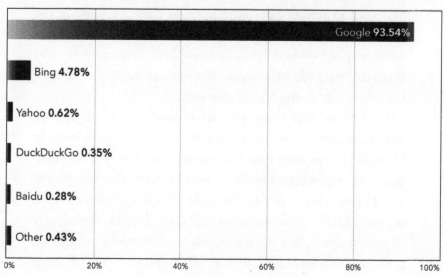

Search engine market share Australia from Aug 2017 – Aug 2018

- Google **93.54%**
- Bing **4.78%**
- Yahoo **0.62%**
- DuckDuckGo **0.35%**
- Baidu **0.28%**
- Other **0.43%**

A look at Google's market share. *Source: StatCounter*

WHAT IS SEO ANYWAY?

Simply put, SEO is the practice of creating greater organic visibility for your website in search engines, driving traffic to your site without paid advertising. It covers a range of activities — both on your website itself and in your surrounding marketing — that are undertaken to optimise a website or web page, to achieve the highest possible ranking in a search engine results page.

Search engines choose how they serve up the results of any particular search query to users, and whether your website or page appears near the top of the list. Your ranking will determine how many people are likely to click through to visit you — in other words, how much traffic you get.

SEO is about understanding the factors that search engines use to make ranking decisions, and leveraging them for your site. Ultimately, a search engine's goal is to provide the best user experience for searchers, so they are looking for indicators — like trust, authority, relevance and even page-loading speed — to determine how likely your site is to help them do that. We have more of a look at the basics of how Google works at the end of this section.

This book will show you what you can do to clearly communicate your website's worth to search engines, namely Google. As I've mentioned, some of these activities will take place on your website itself — on the pages that people see and behind the scenes in the code; this is all referred to as on-page SEO. Other activities will take place independently of your website, like guest blogging, social media marketing, influencer marketing and link building. Both on- and off-page SEO techniques will be covered in this book.

From a business point of view, the ultimate aim of a high search engine ranking is to increase the quantity and quality of organic visitor traffic to a website or page, and ultimately reduce the amount that needs to be spent on paid advertising.

THE SCIENCE OF SEO STRATEGY

The beauty of SEO is that while you are ultimately optimising your website for human beings, it is a piece of software – a search engine – that ultimately decides what user experience is best and which web page ends up where in the search result rankings.

This means there is a pure science behind a winning SEO strategy. You are not trying to influence a particular human being, and no politics are involved – just an algorithm. A search engine algorithm may have a strict set of rules – but these rules, if you know them well, can be bent so far that they can appear to be broken to the untrained eye. While nobody knows Google's algorithm rules for sure, SEO specialists have been studying them for years.

The more knowledge and experience you obtain about how search engines work and rank, the better chance you give your business to grab digital real estate that is growing more valuable every second. It isn't easy, but – just like any business or industry with barriers to entry – if you are willing to put in the hard work then you will gain a greater edge over your competition.

You might think you don't have the budget or the resources to match some of the larger players in your market online, but you have other advantages. Your size and flexibility will allow you to move faster than them in an ever-changing online realm – and the speed at which Google and its competitors are moving is rapid.

As I write this, the hierarchy of search engines is evolving due to the rise of voice and AI technology. Over the next few years, will the majority of us be searching with a keyboard? Amazon's Alexa, Microsoft's Cortana, Apple's Siri and a range of other voice assistants have all entered the market and have become a main focus for these giants. Industry web standards are being collaborated on and set for how all search engines are to handle voice queries with the development of the 'speakable' schema markup format. Why? Because everyone knows the power and potential of the web.

– Dallas Rabot,
Head of Product, Pure SEO

YOU HAVE TO BE SEEN TO BE COMPETITIVE

By competitive, I'm not talking here about needing to put on your most menacing 'game face' and take no prisoners — although you can do that if that's the approach you want to take. What I mean is that you need to be seen to make it into anyone's consideration set — they have to know you're there to have the option of choosing you; that's marketing 101.

The reality is that more and more companies are understanding the importance of being seen by their audience, and investing in SEO. Think about how you are watching TV nowadays . . . I would hazard a guess that it's not television in the traditional sense. More and more people are using streaming services such as Netflix, viewing content in a manner that enables them to pause, fast-forward and skip over the ads.

This could be viewed as bad news for advertisers, but it's actually good news for businesses. In a classic case of David and Goliath, many small businesses can now compete with much larger ones, because you no longer have to have a behemoth budget to be spent on television advertising. With digital, you're paying for pixels on a screen; it's more affordable and easier to achieve good results, especially in smaller markets such as Australia and New Zealand.

That said, the mechanics of doing it well have changed. SEO has evolved much like marketing has evolved. Some of the changes have come from Google's algorithm tweaks. Some have come from user behaviour — changes in the way we are searching, which will be explored in chapter 16. However, SEO is still about serving the right results to the right people.

SUCCESSFUL SEO IS REALLY JUST GOOD MARKETING

Back in the early days, it was quite easy to game the system — using white text hiding on white backgrounds and similar tricks in order to achieve better rankings — but we've moved away from the 'Wild West' of SEO to an actual marketing approach that can (and should) be ethical.

I often say that successful SEO is essentially just good marketing, a sentiment that is proven by many of the people doing it well. For example, take Eventfinda, New Zealand's largest and most comprehensive website for events and live entertainment.

James McGlinn, Eventfinda's CEO, maintains, 'The principles of good marketing very much apply in our approach to search. For us it's about differentiating our audiences and gaining a real understanding of their drivers and what is relevant and valuable to them so that we can create the best possible user experience. This is just good practice but, without a doubt, it reflects in our search success.

'SEO was virtually all we did in the way of marketing in our first decade and our New Zealand site attracts 1.3 million visitors a month — almost 90 per cent of whom come through organic search.'

In essence, a lot of it is about making sure you have good content for your users — interesting content that's relevant and valuable. I'll get more into tactics shortly, I promise. But first . . .

HOW TO USE THIS BOOK

You're holding in your hands an accessible, easy-to-understand and practical guide; think of it like your coach or 'how to' resource that will enable you to DIY your SEO. There's a wealth of information about search marketing and search engine optimisation out there, but it can be difficult to sort through it all and work out what is the most relevant to you. This book pulls together what matters for Australia and New Zealand specifically.

You don't have to be a techie to do it, either! Within these pages you'll find lots of actionable advice from both myself and other experts in the industry — as well as real-life dos and don'ts and a few cautionary tales of red flags you'll want to try to avoid.

Work through the book chapter by chapter and you'll have a strategy for SEO for your business, or dip in and out to tackle specific areas of your search marketing. Either way, implement these things and you'll not only generate a positive impact on your website, but hopefully on your business, too.

Understanding the fundamentals is important, but you don't have to do everything in order to appear in Google's search results. It's about picking the things that will have the biggest impact — and about testing and measuring everything, so that you can learn and understand what's working and see continuous improvements over time. Because that's what it's all about. SEO isn't an overnight success, it's a slow burn . . . which brings me to a few quick myths about SEO that I want to dispel before we get started.

Myth 1: You can get onto page 1 of Google really quickly

Some people come to us and say 'I want to be number one on Google for credit cards'. Well, I'm sorry to break it to you, but you're never going to be number one on Google for something like that. SEO, like so much of business, requires a common-sense approach. I'm not saying here that you shouldn't be ambitious, but be realistic about what you can rank highly for in Google's search results, otherwise you're just wasting money.

As an example, if you're a one-man-band insurance broker,

you're not going to rank number one for 'insurance' no matter how good you are, as the large companies are investing significantly in competing for those top spots. You're much better to understand what your customers are actually searching for when they're looking for your service. They're likely to get more specific than just 'insurance'. It could be something more like 'insurance broker Parnell'. Not only is it much easier to rank for that, it's also going to have a much higher success or conversion rate (the rate at which people achieve the quantifiable goal of your site), because of its relevance.

A lot of people approach us with the idea that 'I've got to be number one for [generic broad term]', but there's only that one spot for that one term. However, there are lots of different terms — and different people search in different ways, so it's about understanding who your target market is, and how they are searching.

The other thing to understand here is that there are no shortcuts. And a word of warning: if an SEO agency is promising quick results, they're full of it and you're best to steer clear of them. However, if you do things properly, over time — with a customer-centric approach and an understanding of how Google works — your SEO will have an effect. Gaming the system and getting rankings really quickly through unethical practices is simply not worth it. Google's web-spam team are a bunch of geniuses looking for exactly that kind of thing, constantly updating their algorithm so that the patterns that underhanded methods leave quickly get picked up.

The last point I want to make is that although SEO takes time to work and may not produce flashy returns on day one — unlike a conversion campaign via Google Ads, which sticks you up the top of the list as long as you go on paying for it — you're getting people to engage with your brand, and that's valuable. It also means that you don't have to pay for all your traffic, like you do via advertising. Not only that, but people who are seeing your search-marketing efforts may not be pushed down a conversion path straight away, but they have the opportunity to engage with your brand on their own terms, often numerous times, and are likely to convert further down the track.

From our perspective at Pure SEO, the customers we sign from organic SEO versus paid advertising stay much longer, and I think that's because of that lengthier sales cycle. They interact with the brand over time; they might come to a blog then sign up to a newsletter, and once we get them they're keepers. Not many people measure conversion rates and the lifetime value of a customer through the different sources of traffic, but it tells a clear story for us.

Broadband comparison site Glimp is another great example of this. Launching in January 2016 and largely DIYing their SEO (with a little help later in the piece from Pure SEO), they've built a site that receives 95 per cent of its traffic through organic search. 'Search is huge,' co-founder Michael Speight maintains. 'You have to do the hard work — you have to grind and hustle. Like business more generally, this is not about the path of least resistance. There are no shortcuts.' Similarly to my final point above, Speight also maintains that organic search traffic is an extremely valuable channel. 'It's behaviour- and intent-driven, so it converts incredibly well compared to display ads or the like.'

Myth 2: Google Ads (paid search) impacts on SEO

Sorry to break it to you, but this simply isn't the case; they are mutually exclusive. If you spend money on Google Ads, that doesn't mean that you're going to rank higher organically. It's not a case of Google looking favourably on the fact that you've placed ad spend with them, so therefore then elevating your organic results — you still have to do the hard yards from an SEO perspective.

Myth 3: When you're ranking top, you can stop

You can, but it might burst your bubble to learn that this then means that you won't stay in your highly coveted and hard-earned top spot forever — or even for long. Your fight to get to the first page requires your constant commitment to remaining there. You have to defend your patch.

Michael Speight of Glimp agrees: 'Just like it takes time and fighting tooth and nail to get to the top one or two spots, it would take that time again to get back up if you're knocked off. You certainly can't rest on your laurels. Our position on that first page is too valuable to us.'

As you'll see in our own case study that's explored (among those of other organisations) throughout this content, SEO is not something you achieve and then just tick off the list. However, it does get easier. Maintenance is easier than working your way up the rankings.

Myth 4: Writing loads and loads of content is going to be better

We're going to explore content more fully in chapters 5 and 6, but I feel that it's important to put a stop to this common misconception right now. Myth 4 is simply not true: more content is not always better. It is true that long-form content ranks better than short-form, but higher-quality content is far preferable to pure volume.

From an SEO perspective, approximately 2000+ words is the optimum length for a piece of content on a website. Part of Google's algorithm is about ranking content based on what it offers in terms of expertise, authority and trust — the building of which is done more successfully in a longer piece. Answer the questions that your customers are asking in a really in-depth way, as opposed to repeating the same one-paragraph spiel that everyone else is using, and you're well on your way.

HOW GOOGLE WORKS

At its most basic level, Google looks at the content on a website to understand what it is about. There are various places on a website that are more important for giving Google these clues, and we'll delve more deeply into those in chapter 2.

Although you know them as your trusty search engine, it pays to think of Google as what it truly is — a business. And as a business, it's there to serve its customers: the world's browsers. Through this lens, we can understand that Google wants to give the best and most relevant information to users as quickly as possible. It employs programmers to write algorithm after algorithm that determine how to supply the best information to searchers. Google is concerned primarily with the experience, after all.

If you do a search and you get something that's irrelevant to you, you're not going to keep coming back. If you do a search and get something really relevant, you've had a good experience; that's what Google wants to promote, as that's what gets its audience. Not everyone comes into a website on the homepage. You come into a website on the most relevant page for what you've searched. Google really cares about relevancy.

This is also why we've seen so many shifts towards more user-based features, as opposed to technical features, in SEO-land. Sure, getting the basics right and in place is important, but this is good news overall for anyone wanting to DIY their SEO. It's helpful to know that actually just bringing some common sense and understanding of the human experience to your SEO will set you in good stead here.

There's so much more I could say, but we've got a whole book for that. For now, let's get into it!

PART ONE: ON-PAGE SEO

ONE:

KEYWORDS: THE FOUNDATION OF SEO

There are probably going to be concepts that I will introduce to you throughout the course of this book that are new to you: keywords is probably not one of them. SEO expert or not, most of us have at least the vague notion that keywords are an intrinsic part of anything related to search. However, knowing that and doing keywords well are two different things.

While it's nice to be starting somewhere that's somewhat familiar, that's not the only reason that keywords form the basis of chapter 1. It's also because keywords play a pivotal role as the foundation of all search marketing; they pretty much underpin everything when it comes to search.

At the most basic level, keywords define your content, and inform search engines and the people searching on them. Think about it this way: when you search for something online — or, when someone searches for your business, service or product — the phrase or string of words you type (keywords) is analysed by search engines and used to return the most accurate and desirable results. (Well, that's the plan, anyway!)

SEARCHING OUTSIDE THE SEARCH BOX: THE PROBLEM WITH PRIMARY KEYWORDS

You may think that your relevant keywords are obvious, but I can assure you the land of keywords is not as straightforward as most of us would like to think. In fact, the most common problem people encounter when choosing keywords is believing that they know what their target market is searching for. You do know your business, after all. It turns out, though, that that's not all there is to keywords.

Consider this example: you have a business (and, of course, a corresponding website) that sells handmade socks with custom designs inspired by 90s cartoons. You have a fairly niche product and — congratulations! — you'll make a lot of geeks incredibly happy, but only if they can find you.

The problem is that very few people will open Google and type 'handmade socks with custom designs inspired by 90s cartoons'. Instead, they might search for 'cool socks' or 'awesome socks' or 'anime socks', or any number of search terms that aren't the exact words you might assume people would enter; those terms that perfectly sum up your product or service.

Perhaps your ideal customer isn't even searching for socks, but instead they're looking for 'cool 90s gift ideas' or 'what to buy my gamer boyfriend for Christmas'. I imagine you're starting to see how this whole 'keyword choosing' thing gets a tad more complicated . . . This doesn't mean that your ideal search term doesn't exist, nor that you won't make a killing once the customer finds your page, it's just unfortunately not how most people search online.

Now, imagine you sell a common product that isn't so niche. Perhaps your business is focused on network security, or cloud computing; maybe you run an aged-care clinic, or are in charge of a small dental practice specialising in cosmetics or orthodontics. How can you compete with the most popular pages that constantly achieve a high ranking for the terms 'network security' or 'dental clinic'? Especially when you consider that the internet is also the playing field of large corporations with an established history of customers and a rich database of information. Here again we see why you need to think beyond your primary keywords — or, rather, think laterally about what your keywords actually are.

RESEARCH PREVENTS YOUR CUSTOMERS FROM RE-SEARCHING

Discovering your ideal keywords — the ones that will perform well for your unique business — requires you to do some research. This won't involve years of dedicated study and poring over thousands upon thousands of pages of search results looking for a magic word that you can capture your audience with, but it will take time, persistence and a little bit of out-of-the-box thinking.

Think of it this way: with search results, it's not about ranking for what you want — it's about ranking for what your customers are searching for. Consider that every time the average person wants to find something, they'll search the first term or phrase that pops into their head. If they don't find it, they'll alter that search a little until, perhaps five results pages later, they settle on the closest product they can find — or, worse, they give up, thinking the product they're looking for doesn't exist.

Understanding the primary keywords you want to rank for is the foundation of your journey to being found online.

It's where you can essentially distil all the information on your website down to a few, core terms. In the case of our boutique sock company above, this might be as simple as Socks, Cartoons, 90s Fashion, Handmade Clothing and Custom Designs.

Once you've thought through the keywords you wish you could rank for — the ones that define your business — then you can look at what we refer to as 'long-tail keywords'.

PINNING THE TAIL ON YOUR KEYWORDS

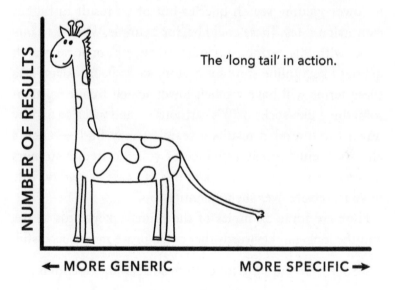

The 'long tail' in action.

NUMBER OF RESULTS

← MORE GENERIC   MORE SPECIFIC →

Singular keywords like those listed above will often be very difficult and time-consuming to rank for — especially for a small or medium-sized business. While these keywords might have extraordinary volume, the competition can be so high that your page can take years before it even reaches page 2 of

Google, which — let's be honest — means it may as well not be there at all.

> There is a joke amongst the SEO community:
>   Where do you hide a dead body so that no one will find it?
>   Page 2 of Google!

Long-tail keywords, on the other hand, are slightly longer variations of those same keywords that may be included in lower-volume search queries but often result in higher conversion rates. These could be, for example, 'Where to buy socks with 90s cartoons printed on them?', or local search queries like 'Online store for custom socks in Auckland'. As these terms will have a much lower search frequency than something like 'socks' or '90s cartoons' — and will also narrow down the intended results a searcher may find — there's already a much greater chance of your desired customers finding them. It pays to think of this as a case of *quality* visits to your website over sheer quantity, too.

Here are some examples of the primary keywords above, and the long-tail keywords that could prove more successful:

Socks: Online store for custom socks with cool prints

Cartoons: Interesting socks printed with old-school cartoons

90s Fashion: Authentic 90s fashion socks for men

Handmade Clothing: Cheap handmade
clothing and socks in my area

Custom Designs: Where to find socks
with custom designs in Brisbane

FINDING AND REFINING YOUR KEYWORDS

Of course, chances are your business isn't the one I've explored in the example above and you don't make quirky socks. If you do, then you're welcome — there's some free work I've already done for you. For everyone else, however, it's time to look at some of the tools, tips and tricks you can use to nail down your own keywords and start improving your search ranking.

Before you get started, you'll need to set up a keywords worksheet like the one below:

KEYWORDS WORKSHEET				
Keyword(s)	Local search volume	Relevance	Google Ads competition level	Competition (INTITLE)
TOP KEYWORDS				
ALL KEYWORDS				

Source: adapted from Jennifer Grappone & Gradiva Couzin,
Search Engine Optimization (SEO): An Hour a Day, *3rd Edition.*

You can create your own keywords spreadsheet in Excel, or download a template from pureseo.co.nz/seobooktools

KEYWORD RESEARCH TOOLS

There are lots of different tools you can use to undertake keyword research, from Google Keyword Planner, which is free to those who advertise via Google Ads, and WordStream, which has a free alternative to its paid service, to paid tools like the Moz Keyword Explorer and SEMrush. Here we have chosen to use the Google Keyword Planner, because most people will have free access to it. It will function in the same way and give you the same data as other similar offerings.

USING A KEYWORD PLANNER

Once you've set up your planning spreadsheet, write down every keyword you think you might like to rank for. It might take five minutes; it might take five hours. No matter how extensive the list is, write down every term, word or phrase you want searchers to type to find your page at the top of the results. Ask staff, customers and other people who know your business for terms they would use to find what you do.

Once you've got your list, enter all of them into Google Keyword Planner. Export your results as an Excel file and copy them into your keywords worksheet, to populate the columns for average search volume and competition level on Google Ads of each term. Note that you will need a Google Ads account to use the Keyword Planner.

Order them by search volume. Remove any terms with zero search volume — there's no point optimising for terms that

KEYWORD	AVG. MONTHLY SEARCHES		COMPETITION
Father's day	2,740,000		Low
Gifts for men	1,830,000		High
Socks	1,830,000		High
Men's socks	1,220,000		High
Women's socks	1,000,000		High
Gifts for women	823,000		High
Gifts for mum	673,000		High
Gifts for dad	673,000		High
Mother's day gifts	550,000		High
Compression socks	550,000		High

no one is actually looking for! At this point the focus is on honing down your giant list of terms to the ones that people are actually searching for.

Next, sort the remaining terms for relevancy: high, medium and low. This is subjective, based on your knowledge of your business. Think about whether a keyword is likely to be entered by a customer of yours, or if the term is actually not that relevant to your target market.

Get rid of anything that you deem to be low in relevancy. Remember, we're finding the most accurate way of answering your customers' search queries, not trying to verify and support your assumptions about how your customers search.

INTITLE SEARCH

Now that you have a slightly shorter list, you can perform an Intitle search. Open up Google and type: Intitle:"your keyword or search term here". Make sure there are no spaces between 'intitle:' and the opening of the double speech marks. Then put in the term and close the speech marks (as per the image below).

This will tell you how many people have this keyword or search term in their page title tag in the exact order you've listed, which gives you an indication of competition. From an SEO perspective, the title tag, or meta title, is the single most important thing on a website. We will describe more about how title tags work at the start of chapter 2 but, suffice it to say for now, if someone is using this term in their title tag, you know they are targeting it from an SEO perspective.

Enter the number of people targeting each term (44,500 in the example above) into your ever-refining spreadsheet of search terms, under the column 'Competition INTITLE'.

LANDING PAGE

Online behaviour now dictates that Google will send a searcher to the *most relevant page* on a website, not necessarily the homepage. Most visitors no longer come in through a site's homepage and navigate to the correct page from there — instead, Google wants them to get the most appropriate page delivered in the search results. So you have to identify which pages are most appropriate for which keywords within your list.

The final column on the spreadsheet, therefore, is 'landing page'. In here, enter the most appropriate page on your website for that particular term, based on the content of each specific page.

Let's consider our sock-company example and the search term '90s cartoons' that we've already explored. Ideally, you want people searching this to be able to come into your site and onto a page that contains just the socks that relate to, and are inspired by, 90s cartoons. You've got other socks on your site, sure — but visitors who want 90s cartoon socks aren't going to want to wade through the rest of them, so they need to land somewhere where what they're looking for is already aggregated.

If there is no appropriate page already on your website that relates to the keyword you've chosen to target, write 'content opportunity' in this column. Flagging these opportunities to add new pages will help when it comes to planning your content strategy later.

After all of that, take a breath — you've earned it. However, don't start to rest on your laurels just yet. While the bulk of the hard work as far as determining your keywords is behind you now, it's worth checking in with your keyword research regularly, as things will change as internet use (and the way we search) continues to evolve. For example, subtle shifts are already occurring as a result of an increase in voice search (we'll explore this further in chapter 16). Just remember, it's worth regularly checking back in on your top terms and any peripheral ones you could be using.

BUILDING ON THE FOUNDATION OF YOUR SEO STRATEGY

Your keywords worksheet should now contain a few key elements:

» keyword search relevancy

» title tag and Google Ads competition level

» relevant landing pages on your website.

KEYWORDS WORKSHEET					
Keyword(s)	Search volume (NZ)	Relevance	Google Ads competition level	Competition (INTITLE)	Landing page
TOP KEYWORDS					
90s cartoons	3400	High	Medium	16,600	teamsockit.co/products/cartoonsocks
Novelty socks	8700	High	High	44,500	teamsockit.co/products
Custom socks	1200	High	Low	22,000	teamsockit.co/products/designyourown
ALL KEYWORDS					
Unique gifts	5200	Medium	High	14,789,342	teamsockit.co/products
Present for Dad	4100	Medium/High	High	456,000	teamsockit.co/products/fathersday
Marvel socks	650	High	Low	3300	content opportunity (superhero socks?)

Looking at the information on your spreadsheet, your top keywords should reveal themselves naturally. What you should be looking for is a good search volume, high relevance and a reasonable level of competition.

Seeing your keywords laid out like this will make it obvious which areas will produce the best results. While it might seem basic or oversimplified — and perhaps a little counterintuitive — all of this is based on what your customers are actually searching for.

Armed with this information, you can compare the keywords you need to rank for with pages on your website that don't exist yet. Check off what you think you're covering well and use this information as the basis of a content gap analysis. Seeing the places where relevant and related content is missing will help you to form a content calendar that you can use to build your site and content into a well-rounded and formidable search engine competitor.

This search volume and competition document will be the foundation of everything you build upon in the coming days, weeks, and months; everything that we explore in the remainder of this book. Even years from now, when you are a master of SEO and can barely remember this moment, all of your success in the online search realm will have started right here and now, with a simple spreadsheet and a few free online tools. The road to get there might be winding and long, but it will also be paved with knowledge, success and continual growth.

Once you've created a list of your top keywords, it's time to look at your website. Keywords are critical — there's no doubt about that — but to use an extended metaphor, they are like the key to a car. That car can't run without the key in the ignition. But without the car, there's nothing for the key to do. Your website is the car, and just like an actual car, it's a complex piece of technology.

TOP TIPS

» Doing keyword research is the foundation of your SEO efforts. Try and look at as many terms as possible.

» Persevere and don't lose hope – the results of your keyword planning investigation might not seem ideal or what you expected, but they are what your customers want.

» Think what your customers may search for, not expecting them to automatically know your industry jargon.

» Reach your local audience – make sure you include geographic-based keywords.

CHAPTER SUMMARY

» Your keywords are the foundation of everything
you will do in the search sphere, but determining
what they are – or should be – is not as
straightforward as one often imagines.

» Think laterally about what your keywords actually
are: the way that you refer to what you do or
sell may not be what other people would type
into a search field in order to find you.

» Think beyond just your primary keywords and
consider how long-tail search terms can work for you.
These typically have lower overall search volumes
but higher conversion rates, meaning people are
more likely to buy, click, respond or otherwise
engage as a result of these more specific queries.

» Research matters – engage with the tools
available online and get input from a range
of people who know your business.

» Using your research, analyse your keywords
based on competition, frequency and relevancy,
to determine where you have a chance to achieve
a high ranking. These are the top terms that will
form the foundation of your SEO strategy.

TWO:

ANATOMY OF A WEB PAGE

You need a well-built website if your keywords are going to take you anywhere. This chapter explores the anatomy of a website, primarily from the end user's perspective. (In chapter 3, the focus will shift onto the inner workings behind the scenes.) It's time to dig a little deeper into the individual aspects of your website, and look at why each and every piece of data on your page is important.

Let's start at the top, and go from there.

META TITLE

Metadata technically refers to any and all of the information that a search engine receives that visitors to your website won't see. This might sound like it goes against what we're covering in this chapter, but a couple of the core elements that relate to SEO do push visible content through to the search results: the meta title and the meta description.

On your website CMS (content management system), the meta title and description tags are usually easy to find and fill in. As an example, the WordPress Yoast SEO plugin, showing meta title and meta description, looks like this:

Snippet Preview

This is a rendering of what this post might look like in Google's search results. Learn more about the Snippet Prev

Auckland SEO | Search Engine Optimisation Auckland
https://www.pureseo.co.nz › auckland-seo

Pure SEO - Your Search Engine Optimisation provider in NZ's Largest City and Surroundings.

🗖 🖳 ✏ Edit snippet

SEO title   ⊕ Insert snippet variable

Auckland SEO | Search Engine Optimisation Auckland

Slug

auckland-seo

Meta description   ⊕ Insert snippet variable

Pure SEO - Your Search Engine Optimisation provider in NZ's Largest City and Surroundings.

The meta title is your web page's main title, indicated by the <title> element if you're examining the HTML side of things. It's the text that you'll see on your browser's toolbar, as well as the title that will display for the page in search engine results. These few words are a critical part of your page's SEO success — in fact, I often say that they're the single most important thing on your website from an SEO perspective — so don't take them lightly.

Knowing that this title is a critical part of SEO can make it tempting to load it with as many keywords as possible. That's not necessarily the way to do it, especially as the importance of the words you use here are weighted by search engines from left to right. Use your primary keyword, certainly, but don't go wild, and consider the order of the words you've chosen.

One more thing: the maximum character count should be 50, or 60 at an absolute stretch. (Google currently shows titles up to 600 pixels.)

Let's go back to our example from the last chapter, the specialist sock company. The most important keyword needs to be at the front of the title tag. It's a sock company — so it's safe to say that 'socks' is the most important starting point.

Socks

Then, building it out into a sentence, we can use another significant keyword — '90s fashion'.

Socks for 90s Fashion Fans

We're currently at 26 characters, including spaces.

We want to add the company name, so that it stands out clearly in the search engine listing. However, it's also important that we don't put it at the front of the title, as we want whatever search engine is used to prioritise your product or service over the company name. The stylistic choice many companies choose to go for is a vertical bar (|) between the key phrase and the company name.

Socks for 90s Fashion Fans | Team Sock-it

We're up to 41 characters now. All in all, everything's looking good.

Keep in mind that you should not duplicate meta titles. Each page of your website should be different, so every title should also be different. Search engines are not keen on duplicated meta titles — it's like having the same name for more than one chapter in a book — so your search visibility will be negatively impacted if you do this.

It's also very important to ensure that the title tag is relevant to the content on the page. Search engines are smart. If your page is entitled 'Best Bargains in Auckland' in an attempt to capture people's interest, but your page is all about your auto body shop in Hastings, Google is going to pick up this discrepancy, and you're going to drop right down in the rankings.

META TITLE TOP TIPS

—

» Meta titles should be a maximum of 50-60 characters (600 pixels).

» They should be unique for every (yes, every!) page of the website.

» They should be relevant for the page they are written for and contain the specific and most important keywords you want that page to rank for.

» Choose your words in descending order of importance, as search engines weight this information from left to right. Generic terms like locations should be on the right, as should brand names (as you will easily rank for your brand anyway).

META DESCRIPTION

Next up is the meta description — the perfect place to let loose with your marketing flair.

Think about what you see when you look something up online. The listings in your search results will generally follow the formula below:

Socks for 90s Fashion Fans | Team Sock-it

www.teamsockit.co/home

Looking for socks inspired by 90s fashion and old-school cartoons? Team Sock-it has custom socks with cool prints. Check out our full range now!

The first line, as you now know, is the meta title. The second line is the page's URL (or web address). The final section is the meta description. It's there to provide context and information about the link showing up on a search engine, hopefully to encourage the user to click through and decide that you're the company for them.

You've got more room to play with the wording for the meta description than the meta title. There's no right answer when it comes to the perfect length for a meta description — Google tweaks what is visible on the search engine results page from time to time. A description of between 120–160 characters is ideal. Sometimes Google will show a different snippet from your page, if there's something not quite kosher with the meta description you've set up.

Make use of your primary keyword/s again, but make sure

the copy around them is engaging and written in an active voice, to ensure people pay attention. You can potentially get in another keyword or two, but err on the side of caution — it's better to have a couple of quality keywords in there surrounded by bubbly copy than stuff it full of keywords that make no grammatical sense when strung together. That's not going to reflect well on your site.

As with the meta title, the meta description should be unique on every page. Otherwise, anyone reading over your listings in the search results will have every reason to think that each page that's popping up is the same as the last one. Create something tailored and appropriate to the page in question, and you'll be set up to do better from the get-go.

While the meta title has a direct correlation to your website's search engine ranking, the meta description has only an indirect impact on it. When you do a search, Google has an idea of the percentage of people who will click on each position (more than half will click on the top three results). However, if your meta description is really good and entices a user to click on you more than Google thinks your position warrants, Google will begin to rank you higher, as it believes users are interested in what you have to say.

HEADERS

Once you've got the title sorted and the meta description organised, it might feel as though the critical parts of your SEO set-up are done. Alas, that's not the case. Sure, the meta title and the meta description are the parts that show up on Google's listings, but actually getting to the front page of Google requires further effort in a large number of areas.

The first place to look at after sorting the meta data is your headers, starting things off with your H1 header. You can set these headers in your content management system (such as WordPress — or whatever system you are using).

The HTML H1 tag refers to the main heading on a website. For example, if you're looking at a single blog post, the H1 will generally be the title of the blog entry, in large and hard-to-miss text at the top of the page. The text in an H1 tag is important for whoever is reading the page — it's likely the first thing that will catch their eye — but it's arguably even more important for search engines, for whom the H1 is a significant ranking factor.

Your H1 should be the first text on the page, with the exception of a menu bar up the top. You should have only one H1 per page, and it should contain the most important information about the subject of the page, in around about 50 characters — give or take 20 characters in either direction.

You may be wondering about the fact that you just created a 50-character phrase for your page when you wrote your meta title. Though that is certainly true, your meta title and your H1 should be different, as they are achieving slightly different aims.

The meta title is designed to entice people to come onto your website when faced with pages and pages of Google results with alternative options. The H1, however, is there to let people know what they are about to read when they are already on the site. It's also another opportunity for optimisation, so sticking to the same script for both the H1 and the meta title means you're losing out on the chance to articulate better to your audience.

The first tier of subheadings is — you guessed it — H2. This should cover themes or sub-topics. Below the H2 is the H3 and then H4, which gets down into more nitty-gritty keywords. This is just like you would see in a Word document with levels of headings and subheadings. The H tags should be in order, and repeated if needed:

H1
- H2
    - H3
    - H3
        - H4
        - H4
- H2
    - H3
        - H4
- H2
    - H3

And so on . . .

Most websites only get as far as H3 on any one page, but you can work your way down to H6 if you require that level of detail on your web page.

One final note on headings: if there is something you want to have up the top looking big and beautiful text-wise, but it doesn't fit the mould of what you should include in an H1, that's OK. You can include it — just don't H1 tag it, instead save the tagging for the appropriate text that is still near the top of the page.

ANCHOR TEXT LINKING

Anchor text is something that most of us interact with every day, even if we don't realise it. It's the text that is displayed in a hyperlink, which takes us to another page when clicked. As you're hopefully coming to realise by now, as with so much else on a web page, there are ways of making small changes to your anchor text to improve your SEO outcomes.

Frequently you'll see hyperlinks indicated with 'click here' or 'visit this page' as their text. While this may have made sense in the early days of internet use — when clicking on hyperlinks wasn't yet second nature — these days, it would be rare to find a person using the internet who isn't comfortable with basic principles like linking.

So much of SEO comes down to careful word usage in the right places — and this is no exception. 'Click here' is as generic as it gets, and generic text isn't going to do you any favours. Instead, go for something to-the-point and relevant to your keywords. More specifically, it needs to be relevant to the keywords relating to the page it is linking to.

Let's imagine that your website has an information page about the eco-friendly and sustainable factory where your socks are manufactured.

Instead of:

Click here to learn about where we make our socks!

A better option might be:

Learn about our sustainable sock manufacturing.

It's succinct, it matches the primary focus of the page it links to, and it will hopefully pique the interest of both human browsers and web crawlers.

IMAGE OPTIMISATION – ALT ATTRIBUTES

Images are a powerful addition to any web page — we all know a picture's worth a thousand words, or so the saying goes. But while an image might have that thousand-word effect on actual humans using the site, things go a little differently when search engines are crawling your site and deciding where it should rank. All the beautiful scenery and cute puppies in the world won't make a bit of difference to your ranking if you haven't optimised your images for SEO — and that's where alt attributes come in.

Outside of SEO, alt attributes are a key part of the internet experience for those who use screen readers to browse the internet. These devices are used by blind and visually impaired people, and they basically read out the text on a page to the user. When they come to an image, however, the technology isn't at a point where it can interpret that for the user — so an alt attribute provides a description or explanation of what is in the image, e.g. yellow cotton socks.

Google places a high value on the content of these alt tags, so it's a great place to pop in your keywords again, if appropriate. Google often uses these words to determine what to show in a Google image search.

'Appropriate' has been a recurring word in this chapter — but it's important to remember. Don't try to game the system with keyword stuffing — just be sensible and work within the parameters of what Google and other search engines like so as to make the most of your time spent on SEO. Ultimately, that's all any of us can do!

Let's imagine our booming sock business again. Perhaps you have an image of a pair of Pokemon socks as part of an article on anime fashion trends. Your alt text could read: 'Image of 90s fashion socks with Pokemon cartoon design from Team Sock-it'. You've got your keywords, you've got your description, you're good to go.

BREADCRUMBS

Remember the fairy tale of Hansel and Gretel? Not the part about the witch and the oven, but the part about the breadcrumb trail they left behind them so they could find their way home. Of course, in the story, a little bird ate the crumbs and they got lost in the woods. Not ideal.

But the idea of a breadcrumb trail has stuck around — sans the hungry bird. In user design (designing the website with the user's journey in mind), breadcrumbs are a series of words near the top of the web page that remind the user where they are within the larger website.

For example, you might see something along the lines of:

Home > Apparel > Socks > Animal Socks

This not only shows you where you are, but the words also function as links that allow you to easily go back a level. For example, if you'd inadvertently clicked Animal Socks when you'd intended to select Superhero Socks, you just need to click 'Socks' in the breadcrumbs in order to go back to where you came from.

However, we're here to talk through SEO, not just web-design components. As with many other aspects of design that we have already mentioned, while there's an underlying purpose that this element fulfils, there are also ways to consider this element of the page from an SEO perspective.

First of all, breadcrumbs are beneficial when considering bounce rate — those people who land on your website and then leave without viewing any other pages — as they create a positive experience for first-time visitors to your website. For example, you may have come onto the page for a pair of Cartoon Zebra Socks. But through the breadcrumbs at the top of the page, you can see where you are, and easily navigate to see a range of related products:

Home > Apparel > Socks > Animal
Socks > Cartoon Zebra Socks

There's one thing we could be doing better with the breadcrumb language, however. Remember that this is sitting near the top of the page, in prime territory for Google and other search engines to sweep through. 'Apparel', 'Socks', 'Animal Socks', etc are all important phrases to be using, as they are the core defining characteristics of each page. 'Home', however, is not such a useful word to include when keywords could be utilised instead. Options could include:

NZ Sock Specialists > Apparel > Socks >
Animal Socks > Cartoon Zebra Socks

Or perhaps:

Online Sock Shop > Apparel > Socks >
Animal Socks > Cartoon Zebra Socks

Work through your keywords and key phrases and you should find something that fits (excuse the pun).

ROBOTS.TXT

You read that correctly — the next area to look at involves robots. In a manner of speaking, of course. Web robots are pieces of software that run automated tasks on the internet. The relevant ones for you are the web crawlers or web spiders that analyse and file information from all over the internet at incredible speed. They're the foundation of how search engines operate.

But you might have pages that you want these robots to crawl more than others. There may be pages that you don't want them to touch at all — perhaps a staging site for a new-look website that's not ready to influence your search engine ranking just yet. Maybe some pages are important for you to have on your website, but the content isn't necessarily as useful on those pages as on others, and you don't want Google to decide your ranking based on that content.

Keep in mind, though, that if there are links going off from a page that you've blocked from being crawled, and those links aren't found anywhere else on your website, those linked pages won't be crawled either.

It's probably best to ask your website developer to create your robots.txt file. However, most common CMS have the ability to create and edit this file.

To find out if your website has a robots.txt file, type your website into the browser followed by robots.txt. For example, to do this for our business, we would enter:

www.pureseo.co.nz/robots.txt

This should bring up a page that looks like this:

The term 'user-agent' means the above-mentioned robot. The * indicates that this message is for all robots. The next line details the pages that we do not want the robots to crawl, scan, look at or put in their index. In the case above, we do not want robots to look at the admin login page for our website. If we let Google index our CMS login page and a potential customer found it they would immediately click away, as there's nothing for them in there!

The final line tells Google (and other robots) where our sitemap is situated. The robots.txt we have has been auto-generated by the Yoast plugin in WordPress.

HTTPS

That's HTTP*S* — and it's not just a plural of HTTP. These days, that 'S' is incredibly important when it comes to being considered for the top-ranking spots by Google.

You are probably familiar with seeing http:// at the beginning of a web address or URL. What you may not have noticed is that over the past few years, more and more sites have started to have https:// instead of http://.

HTTP stands for 'Hypertext Transfer Protocol', while HTTPS is 'Hypertext Transfer Protocol Secure'. For the most part, they are the same — except for that little extra touch of security.

In the past, Google had encouraged companies to switch over to HTTPS by providing a small ramp-up in ranking for websites that migrated over. Now, however, it's a critical move to make, as Google is marking any site with HTTP as 'not secure', which is the last thing you want a first-time visitor to your site to see. It's also not going to help you get found via search engines. Non-secure/HTTP websites are shown in the Chrome browser as follows:

ⓘ Not secure

So the bump in ranking, plus the fear of your website being marked as 'not secure', are both sufficient factors to make sure that if you haven't migrated yet, you do it as soon as possible. It can be a hefty job, so make sure you consult with professionals unless you're really confident in your web-development abilities.

CONTENT

It seems ridiculous to mention content so far through this chapter. Content is king, so they say. But in this instance, it's only a passing reference — the chapters on content creation are further along.

It's worth bringing up content at this point, however, to discuss where it sits in this exploration of the anatomy of a web page. Here are a few key tips to get you started:

CONTENT TOP TIPS

» Stay on topic – both in the general sense and the keyword sense. If your blog post starts out packing in phrases like 'best plumber in the Waikato' and 'drain unclogging', but then becomes a treatise on how much you want to buy a boat, Google's not going to like that.

» Sprinkle your keywords throughout your content, and keep your overarching purpose in mind. After all, you want this page to target a specific searcher's intent, and they want to feel like they got what they wanted (or ideally more) when they eventually navigate away from the page.

» If appropriate, find sections of your text with keywords and link these through to relevant pages on your site. The best way to think about this is: as a website visitor, would this link be useful for me? If the answer is yes, link away.

SITE STRUCTURE

All of these separate parts add together to create your website. In order to really take it to the next level, it's also crucial to consider the actual structure of your site. At the heart of this structural success is SEO siloing, a concept created by Bruce Clay — one of the most respected SEO practitioners in America.

In a general business sense, siloing is something many organisations are trying to avoid these days — instead, they are trying to crosspollinate between divisions and ensure that employees have a view of the business beyond their own limited area. However, in SEO, siloing is a key part of making sure that you can prove to search engines that you have enough appropriate keyword-supported material to warrant a high ranking.

What's more, siloing also enhances the user experience and helps people who are browsing the website — not just the web crawlers from Google and the like. It's a real-life modern-day example of divide and conquer.

Think of it this way: if there's no clear thematic structure to the content on your site, search engines are going to identify it as a vague sum of its parts. Cartoon socks, for example. Useful, certainly, but not as specific as it could be. That's one specific topic to rank for — but couldn't there be more?

After successful siloing, Google might understand that there are actually four different themes that your website ought to rank for: Anime Socks, Superhero Socks, Animal Socks and Silly Socks. Each silo will require at least five content pages in order to really establish the theme. Perhaps it's different item pages within the theme, or blog content that is specifically related to that theme. The specific ways in which siloing can be executed will depend on the type of business and type of website that you have.

CHAPTER SUMMARY

» Meta titles are the single most important thing on your web page from an SEO perspective. However, there are other aspects of your website's 'anatomy' that you can make the most of.

» Your meta description exists to provide context and information about your website or page. It's your chance to encourage searchers to click through, so don't waste it.

» The H1 header is different to your meta title; think of it as a 'you are here' description on your web page.

» Internet users are now far more comfortable with the concept of links, so make the anchor text for your link something more relevant (and keyword optimised) than the old-fashioned 'click here'.

» Images can be optimised, too – look to the alt attributes for another optimisation option.

» Lay a navigable trail of 'breadcrumbs' through your site for maximum usability and search optimisation.

» Robots that crawl the internet are automated scripts that crawl websites to gather information,

and you can have a say in how they behave
on your site with the robots.txt file.

» Switch to the safer and more secure HTTPS protocol
to avoid penalties when it comes to search ranking.

» Content that is relevant, on topic and contains just
a sprinkling of keywords is the most effective.

» Having everything operating only within its
individual silo might not be ideal for your business,
but it's good for the structure of your website.

THREE:

ANATOMY OF 'BEHIND THE PAGE'

It's one thing to understand the elements on the page that you can see — it's another to wrap your head around what's going on 'behind' the page. In this chapter, we peer further behind the curtain.

Somewhat contrary to popular belief, the lion's share of things going on behind the scenes and in the deep dark depths of web-development code aren't directly related to SEO. Those elements can be left to the dedicated web developers, rather than taking up valuable real estate in this book. I'll keep things short and sweet.

CONTENT MANAGEMENT SYSTEMS (CMS)

A content management system (CMS) is a system that allows a non-technical user to control and manage what appears on their website. Some of the main SEO tactics in this book will be able to be implemented via your CMS: things like meta data, adding content to the website, creating new pages and even tagging images. Most CMS are quite similar; if you become familiar with one, you are likely to pick up the others quite quickly.

There are broadly two types of CMS: proprietary and open-source. An open-source CMS is one that has the source code freely available to anyone. These are popular because there is no upfront cost involved to use or modify it. While you may still pay a web developer to set you up a website using one of these CMS, the software itself carries no price tag and you have the option of then doing your own modifications and additions to your site at no cost.

A proprietary CMS is one where the website developer has coded or created their own CMS. Proprietary software is sometimes in place for a specific industry, for example hospitality, and carries a licensing fee. However, it is much more common for websites to use an open-source CMS.

Another benefit of choosing an open-source CMS is that website developers are continually creating and releasing plugins. These plugins are often free and can be installed to allow extra functionality on your CMS. If you are using WordPress (which is by far the most popular CMS), you should install the Yoast SEO plugin. This is the most common way to edit your 'behind the page' SEO elements, which we'll explore in more detail now.

CMS TOP TIP

Unless you need a large, expensive bespoke website, it is always advisable to go for an open-source CMS. With an open-source solution there will be lots of developers who are familiar with the CMS, which means you can change developers freely. With a proprietary CMS it is much harder to change developers; in fact, you may not actually even own your own website!

The top 10 open-source CMS are:

#	WEBSITES USING	MARKET SHARE %	ACTIVE SITES	# OF WEBSITES IN MILLION
1	WordPress	59.9 %	26,701,222	239,139
2	Joomla	6.6 %	2,009,717	13,480
3	Drupal	4.6 %	964,820	23,330
4	Magento	2.4 %	372,915	12,095
5	Blogger	1.9 %	758,571	15,779
6	Shopify	1.8 %	605,506	11,587
7	Bitrix	1.5 %	200,210	3,925
8	TYPO3	1.5 %	582,629	3,568
9	Squarespace	1.5 %	1,390,307	9,799
10	PrestaShop	1.3 %	262,342	2,099

Source: https://websitesetup.org/popular-cms/

BEHIND-THE-PAGE SEO ELEMENTS

CANONICALIZATION

It's definitely a tongue-twister of a word, but it's hopefully not such a complex concept to wrap your head around, once you've got the necessary information.

Different people will take different approaches when typing in a URL to get to the same page. Think about it: https://www.teamsockit.co and http://teamsockit.co, for example, would take you to the very same page. So would the variations http://www.teamsockit.co and https://teamsockit.co. That's before we even get into more complicated possible variations like http://www.teamsockit.co/home. The possibilities aren't quite endless, but they are certainly many and varied.

https://www.teamsockit.co

https://teamsockit.co

https://www.teamsockit.co/index.php

https://teamsockit.co/index.php

https://www.teamsockit.co.nz

https://teamsockit.co.nz

https://www.teamsockit.co.nz/index.php

https://teamsockit.co.nz/index.php

Or as another example, your website may have a blog, and that blog has different categories. Some posts may sit in multiple categories, meaning that your one post may have multiple URLs attributed to it.

Let's say we have an article: 'Our 10 top superhero socks to keep you warm this winter'. The post shows up on your main blog page. It would then fit into the blog categories of 'seasonal' and 'superhero', so you add it to both. So there are now three URLs:

https://www.teamsockit.co/blog/10-top-superhero-socks

https://www.teamsockit.co/blog/
seasonal/10-top-superhero-socks

https://www.teamsockit.co/blog/
superhero/10-top-superhero-socks

And they all contain the same post.

There's an issue with this. A regular person browsing the web would consider these to all be the same page — different ways of getting to the same result. However, the web crawlers and robots mercilessly canvassing the internet identify each of these various URLs as different pages — pages with duplicate content. And duplicate content does not have a favourable effect on your search ranking.

There are various takes out there on whether or not Google actively penalises websites for duplicate content — but chances are that other websites will be prioritised. In other words, even if you're not actively getting a penalty, the ultimate result is much the same. Better to err on the side of caution and avoid duplicate content causing issues — and that's where canonicalization comes in.

Put simply, canonicalization is the inserting of a 'canonical' tag into a page's HTML — and that tag is used to identify which version of a duplicate page is the original or master version.

In practice this will look something like this:

```
<link rel='canonical' href='https://www.teamsockit.
co/blog/10-top-superhero-socks'/>
```

It's a simple line of HTML code that sits within the <head> section, where all the page's metadata is stored. I touched on metadata in the previous chapter, when discussing meta titles and meta descriptions, since both of those actively show up either on the page itself or in the search results. Canonical tags, on the other hand, are part of the majority of the metadata that is doing all its legwork behind the scenes.

With canonical tags in place in the code of the appropriate duplicate pages, you're doing yourself a favour, regardless of any penalties that may be at play. Think of it this way: instead of diluting your ranking potential across multiple different pages, all search engine energy will be focused in on that one master version. This is better than it sharing the love between however many variations there might be out there. You'll rank higher this way regardless of Google's current approach to duplicate content — so it's worth that little extra line of code.

Using the Yoast SEO plugin on WordPress, most canonical tags will be automatically assigned (making it nice and easy). However, if you want to specify your canonical, you can do so under advanced settings:

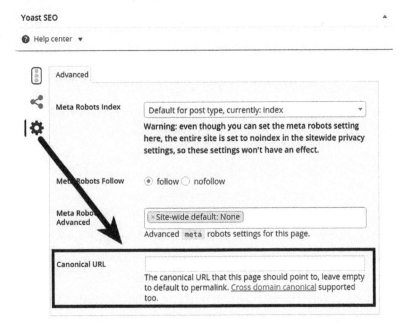

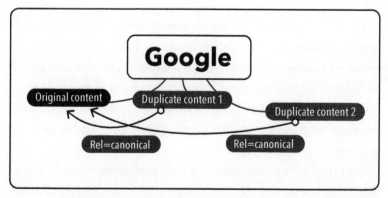

With Rel=canonical tag, Google knows which is the original content

W3C CODE COMPLIANCE

The W3C is the handy short-form name of the World Wide Web Consortium — the same world wide web that gives us www at the start of website URLs. Specifically, the W3C develops the standards of the internet so that there's as much compatibility between different platforms and browsers as possible.

And it's that compliance that's relevant here. Sometimes a web page will load properly on one browser, and not on another. As a general rule of thumb, this can be chalked up to developers not testing it on different browsers, having used code that isn't W3C compliant — either because the consortium has elected not to adopt that element and include it in the standard, or hasn't yet convened on it, if it's a new addition by an industry player such as Google or Mozilla.

Fun fact: W3C is still jointly led by the guy who invented the world wide web, Tim Berners-Lee!

For the most part, unless your website's code is wildly off-base, you shouldn't face major issues — both with your search engine ranking and with the user experience. The one caveat is older machines running Internet Explorer 6, which isn't up to date on the latest HTML standards. However, the number of users worldwide on IE6 is getting smaller and smaller by the day.

You may still potentially run into problems when it comes to any different and exciting things that your browser is newly capable of. Between meetings of the W3C, browser creators will add in new capabilities that they will then push to have added to the standards, ensuring that browsers across the board will play nicely with them.

Ultimately, the good news is that checking for W3C webcode compliance is incredibly straightforward. https://validator.w3.org is a service provided by W3C to do just that — either by simply copying and pasting the URL of the website you wish to check, or by uploading an HTML file from your computer. When it's that easy to check, there's nothing to be lost by doing so. The worst-case scenario is that issues are flagged that need to be fixed — and really, that's important news to hear, since the alternative would be to discover it the hard way, through something malfunctioning badly.

SCHEMA.ORG

Schema — more officially schema.org, but I'll stick with the common usage for now — is a self-described 'collaborative, community activity' between Google, Bing, Yahoo! and Yandex (the biggest search engine in Russia). Put simply, schema allows search engines to show more informative (or richer) search results.

Schema markup is a form of microdata — effectively metadata that sits within the content on the page, rather than with the rest of the regular metadata that all sits at the top of the HTML within the <head> tag.

The purpose of schema is to provide search engines with specific kinds of information that they can use to create an enriched listing.

Pavlova - Taste
https://www.taste.com.au/recipes/pavlova.../e62d3cc8-a69d-4ae3-8a6d-52... ▾
★★★★★ Rating: 4.8 - 90 votes - 2 hrs 45 mins - 460.075 cal
Method. Preheat oven to 120°C. Line an oven tray with foil. Brush with melted butter and dust with cornflour, shaking off excess. Use an electric mixer to whisk egg whites in a clean dry bowl until soft peaks form. Use an electric mixer to whisk the cream and icing sugar in a medium bowl until firm peaks form.

Pavlova - Edmonds
https://edmondscooking.co.nz/recipes/desserts/pavlova/ ▾
The recipe for a lofty meringue cake evolved slowly in both Australia and New Zealand, but the name arrived in 1935 when Bert Sachse, chef at the Esplanade ...

Enriched listings with, and without, schema

In these examples, the first result corresponds to a page that has schema markup. You can see several aspects that Google has elected to display on the search engine results page:

» the rating, in stars and as a number

» the number of people who have posted a rating

» the cook time of the recipe

» the energy in the recipe, indicated in calories.

These little snippets are incredibly useful. The people who click through to this recipe know what they are getting themselves in for. They understand the time commitment, and they know that a fairly large number of people have spoken up in favour of this recipe. The meta description still does its job, but in some ways, it doesn't have to work as hard, as many of the selling points are covered in the schema.

The second link requires more blind trust before clicking through. We know it's a pavlova recipe, and we know it's from Edmonds. But that's about it. In order to find out more, we have to click through — and we may well immediately click away again if we see something that's not in line with what we want.

Of course, people may still click away from the first result anyway — perhaps the steps are too complicated, or there's a tricky ingredient that they don't have to hand. However, with some of those essentials covered in the schema, it's still a safer bet — especially with the review information displayed. Facts and figures are one thing, but validation from the general public is another thing all together!

Including schema doesn't just help your listing pop and your click-through rate increase — it can also help your SEO overall. While it's not a magic ticket to the front page of Google, it helps web crawlers understand the content of your page more effectively. Every bit counts. As you'll have realised by now, there are innumerable moving parts that all play a role in SEO, and schema is only one of them — but a very wise one to make use of. However, it is quite technical and is probably best done by a professional web developer.

CHAPTER SUMMARY

» The majority of behind-the-scenes code on your website isn't directly related to search results, but there are a few things you can optimise.

» Most CMS function in similar ways, although our preference for being able to continually optimise and improve your site for search is an open-source system.

» Use canonicalization to avoid dilution when it comes to search traffic.

» Ensuring you have W3C webcode compliance is essential but, luckily, there's a handy online tool that lets you do that.

» Make use of schema to enrich your search listings and achieve better results.

FOUR:

THE RIGHT INFORMATION, WHERE AND WHEN YOU WANT IT

In today's digital space, in order to be relevant, you have to be mobile. Think about it: when you walk past bus stops, sit on trains or attend events, a large proportion of people are invariably engaged with their mobile devices in one way or another.

Google knows it too — and in March 2018, they began rolling out their mobile-first index; something they have been openly talking about doing since 2016.

In a nutshell, this means exactly what it sounds like: Google is now using the mobile version of a web page or website for indexing and ranking. It's not mobile-only in that a desktop site can still be included, but it will look to mobile-friendliness first when it determines rankings. Effectively, Google are indexing the web via mobile web pages rather than desktop pages — and your mobile version will be considered the primary version of your website.

This move reflects user behaviour. The figures vary depending on the source you refer to, but with time, the proportion of desktop searches to mobile and tablet searches is getting closer and closer to reaching parity and, in many cases, mobile has become the dominant source of searches.

Event and live entertainment site Eventfinda receives more than 1.3 million visits to its website each month, and has tracked behavioural changes around mobile use of its site on both sides of the Tasman. According to its analytics, while only 1.3 per cent of visits to its New Zealand site were made from mobile devices in January 2010, by July 2018 this figure had risen to 67.5 per cent.

In Australia, mobile use started ahead of the (Kiwi) curve, followed by a steep adoption period between mid-2011 (9.6 per cent) and early 2012 (32.5 per cent). However, nowadays the Kiwis and Aussies are fairly equal. Whether you're marketing to searchers on either side of the ditch, these figures indicate that mobile traffic is too significant to ignore.

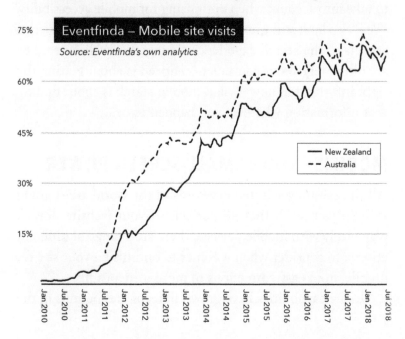

Eventfinda – Mobile site visits
Source: Eventfinda's own analytics

And it's not just our 'social browsing' either; broader metrics tell the same story. According to GlobalStats, in the year ending June 2018, 52.19 per cent of searches in the Oceania region across all sites were made on desktop, versus 38.21 per cent on mobile devices and 9.59 per cent on tablets.

Pure SEO conducted independent research analysing hundreds of Google Analytics accounts across New Zealand and Australia, and found that in 2017 mobile search sessions actually surpassed the volume of search sessions by desktop and tablet.

Whichever way you look at it, if you aren't set up to handle the different ways people search and browse on phones and tablets, you're potentially losing out on almost half of the people out there (maybe more!) — and that number is only going to grow.

In this chapter, we'll work through some of the key things to take into account when optimising for mobile accessibility. We'll also look at the importance of speed in search. These two aspects of the search experience tie together well, since they are ultimately about convenience. Speed is about getting the right information now — and mobile search is about finding that information wherever you happen to be.

MOBILISE YOUR SMALL-SCREEN POWER

All the carefully selected keywords in the world aren't going to help you reach that 48 per cent if your website doesn't play nicely with mobile devices. There are a range of different criteria to consider when it comes to optimising your site for mobile, from easy corrections to more in-depth fixes.

Mobile capabilities have grown in leaps and bounds in the

last few years. These days, most elements of web design can translate in some way to the smallest screens in the house. Once upon a time, numerous elements were best avoided when creating mobile-friendly websites. JavaScript was a big issue, and even seemingly integral components like custom CSS (cascading style sheets — a big part of what makes your site look like you) and imagery provided a challenge for many types of phones and devices.

Today, that's rarely the case. Many mobile nuances these days are down to creating a positive and uncomplicated user experience, rather than limited capabilities. After all, the last thing you want to do is get to the top of search ranking through great keyword usage and content development, only to have people immediately swipe back to Google or Bing to pick another result that is easier to navigate.

The following are a few things to consider doing — or not doing — in order to give your visitors a great experience once they've arrived at your site.

DO: KEEP USERS IN ONE BROWSER WINDOW

While it's fairly straightforward for most users to figure out how to navigate between windows or tabs on a desktop computer or laptop, it's another story on mobile devices. Keep them on one journey, in one window, so that they can swipe back to your homepage easily if needed.

DON'T: USE FLASH FOR FLASHY CONTENT

Flash plugins don't work on all models or operating systems, meaning that some mobile users will miss out on the experience. If adding special effects is critical to your website's look and feel, chances are your web developer will be doing this. However, if you are building these yourself, or want to check that what they're doing will be compatible with mobile, make sure you (or they) are using HTML5 to construct them instead.

DO: STREAMLINE ANY FORMS

When it comes to filling in details, whether it's to sign up for a mailing list or to make a purchase through an e-commerce site, it's important to keep things as straightforward as possible. Think autofill where possible, copying over shipping address content to the billing address fields, and using visual calendars for date selection, so users won't need to leave the browser to consult another calendar.

DON'T: OVERWHELM USERS WITH PROMOS AND POP-UPS

We've all been there — you visit a website on your mobile device and find yourself faced with a full-page pop-up telling you to install their app now. Inevitably, there's a large button shouting 'YES! INSTALL NOW!' and a smaller one with a slightly snarky message. 'I don't like discounts' or 'No thanks, convenience isn't for me'. It's not clever, it's not funny — it's just aggravating to users who genuinely wanted to use your site and now feel much less inclined to do so.

DO: MAKE IMAGES EXPANDABLE

If you're shopping online and browsing through a website's catalogue, you want to get a full picture of what you're potentially going to be spending your hard-earned money on. If you have a retail site, make sure that your products are illustrated with high-quality images that users can zoom in on.

DON'T: FORCE USERS TO NAVIGATE IN ALL DIRECTIONS

Scrolling up and down is fine — necessary, in fact, unless your page is incredibly short. But avoid horizontal scrolling. It's unwieldy, makes text hard to read and generally detracts from the user experience.

TOP TIP

Google specifically penalises sites for horizontal scroll, so be aware of this aspect of design if you want to get to the top of the search-ranking charts.

DO: DESIGN FOR IMPRECISION

Not everyone has perfect aim when using a touch screen. If your web design includes buttons or links that are too big or too small, or includes these elements in the pathway of a scrolling finger, accidental clicks are inevitable. Take into account large fingers and shaky hands.

DON'T: DESCRIBE THE DESKTOP VERSION AS THE 'FULL SITE'

Some users will see the words 'click here for full site' and assume that the mobile version they are currently on is lacking content or options. Then they'll find themselves navigating the desktop site on a mobile device and having a sub-optimal experience in the process. This could be enough of an issue that they will elect to navigate away from your website entirely. Stick to 'desktop version' in your wording.

TOP TIP: THE MOBILE-FRIENDLY TEST

Google takes mobile optimisation seriously. As part of this, they have created a mobile-friendly test tool. It does what it says on the tin: simply enter the URL of the web page you want to test, and Google will let you know if it's up to the job.

After a few seconds of analysing, if everything is suitable, you'll get the green light and a reassuring 'Page is mobile friendly' message.

But if there are issues impacting the mobile experience, you'll be promptly told 'Page is not mobile friendly' in big red letters. The report goes on to identify the problems in plain and simple terms to ensure you can see where attention is required, and provides a screenshot of the site's appearance on the virtual Google phone screen.

In one example, the identified issues were:

» content wider than screen

» text too small to read

» viewport not set

» clickable elements too close together

Thankfully, all of these are things that can be relatively easily remedied. Google even goes so far as to provide resources at the bottom of the report, including links to pages with advice for fixing the errors and reporting on usability issues for the whole website, rather than just the page entered for this initial report. There's also a link to a more general mobile-friendly pages article, and to Google's discussion group forum, which are helpful resources.

HIT THE ACCELERATOR

If you've done some reading around mobile web design and SEO in the past, you may well have stumbled across one particular acronym — AMP.

AMP stands for 'accelerated mobile pages'. The AMP Project is an initiative driven by Google — an open-source technology that exists to improve the performance of web content on mobile devices. Since its announcement in October 2017, AMP has grown to include more than two billion pages globally.

The speed comes from the stripped-back nature of the pages. Effectively, you're taking a site that has already been designed to play well on mobile devices and making it more 'bare bones' to make it load even quicker. The framework is like a simplified (but very strict) version of HTML.

That strict nature of the AMP HTML means that attention to detail is necessary. The pages must be properly validated in order to function every time — and in order to amp up your place in Google's rankings, your AMP site must function every time.

But the effort can pay off. Pages created on the AMP framework boast some impressive figures; according to Google, AMP pages that are linked through search results typically load in less than a second — and they also use 10 times less data than their standard, non-AMP counterparts.

When people have short attention spans, and are conscious of how much data they are using on their phone, it's wise to consider this option. In fact, according to behavioural analytic research by Kissmetrics, 40 per cent of people abandon a web page if it takes over three seconds to load, so it's certainly an option worth investigating. A little extra investment into the design process to create an AMP version could mean a significant boost in sales.

DYNAMIC VS. RESPONSIVE DESIGN

If your website isn't already mobile-friendly, there are many things to think about before diving in to make things right.

One of these is which type of mobile-friendly format you pick. There's no single right answer, but here are a few key points about the differences between dynamic and responsive design so that you can begin to wrap your head around them.

Responsive design, as the name suggests, responds to the nature and dimensions of the device on which it is being accessed. The same code is delivered to the browser, whether you're running Safari on iOS, Edge on Windows, Chrome on Android, or any other combination of operating system and browser. But that code is served up in slightly different ways to fit the display size in question.

It's straightforward to maintain compared to more dynamic options, which in turn makes it relatively inexpensive. However, because the exact same content is appearing on mobile devices as it is on desktops, the experience isn't as tailored for mobile users as it could be — and data-heavy pages may take a while to load.

Dynamic design tailors the site to the device with much more precision. Different HTML and CSS can be used depending on the device in question, meaning that mobile users receive the perfect experience for their devices. Desktop, tablet, mobile . . . your catering to different devices is really only limited to the budget you can put aside for web developers.

Dynamic design is ideal, when circumstances permit. It will have a higher upfront cost, and high ongoing costs to ensure proper maintenance is carried out to keep it up to date. But it also means you can make sure that your users get the experience that you really want them to have.

SPEED DEMONS

In the case of SEO, the speed demons aren't the ones tearing out ahead of the pack — they are the sites where slow loading speed holds them back; think of them as the sort of anti-speed demons if you will. This chapter has already touched on the impact of speed as it relates to users' browsing habits — if it takes too long to load, they'll swipe away — but we are also in an era where Google is penalising slow websites with a ranking algorithm focused on mobile speed.

This algorithm is designed to impact only the slowest of the slow at this stage, but it's a timely reminder that with time, Google is picking up on each and every factor that creates a positive — or negative — user experience, and evolving their search rankings accordingly.

CHAPTER SUMMARY

» Google has rolled out its mobile-first index. If it was only anecdotally important to cater to mobiles before, this has now become even more vital.

» Create your website with mobile in mind, making navigation easy and design uncomplicated, bearing in mind the way users interact with phone screens.

» Speed matters, so beware of anything that will slow down your website's loading speeds.

» There are heaps of great tools available, from checking your website's speed to optimising it for mobile.

FIVE:

COMPREHENSIVE CONTENT

'Content' is a word that simultaneously explains very little but contains a lot. Terms like 'content marketing' and 'content creator' get bandied about all the time, but unless you're actually working in the marketing end of the business space, what these things actually mean can be somewhat of a mystery. Here's a quick round-up of content-related terms you might encounter.

'Content' in this context is information, material, experience. Specifically, it's 'something that is to be expressed through some medium, as speech, writing, or any of various arts' — at least according to dictionary.com. It's the information on a website. Articles on a blog. Podcasts, videos, infographics . . . all content.

'Content creator' simply refers to someone who creates content. They might be focused on blogging or creating videos, but whatever their skill set is, the end goal is creating original material for use online.

'Content marketing' is a specific subset of marketing that is more organic and 'gentle' than traditional promotion-focused marketing. It can include everything from social media posts to videos to blogs, and is designed to stir up interest and provide something useful to the reader/watcher/consumer rather than selling something to them.

'Content curation', as opposed to 'content creation', is the process of gathering together content from other sources and sharing it via social media platforms — for example, if your product was a high-quality vanilla essence, you might share various recipes that would let your product shine. The content creation equivalent would be creating that recipe from scratch.

With those core terms sorted, we can start looking into the broader world of content and its relationship with SEO.

THE MULTITUDES WITHIN CONTENT

Content isn't just writing — as I've already mentioned, material like video and infographics all falls under the content umbrella. But there's a written aspect to all of these kinds of content, whether it's subtitles on a video or captions and alt text on an infographic — and all of these little bits of writing can potentially be harnessed for SEO.

It's important to consider whether to use these different mechanisms of content delivery — and if so, how. We all absorb information and learn in different ways, so for some people, visual delivery is the way to go. Videos, photos, infographics — anything where the point can be presented using imagery. However, these methods of content delivery still need to be discovered or found within search results — and that's where optimising all kinds of content, not just the straight-up written word, comes into play.

BLOGGING BETTER

But first, the tried and true. Blogging is the first port of call for most people starting to build up their content. While not all writers are created equal, if you know what problems you want to be solving with your online content, you can combine that with some appropriate keyword research to start making inroads to great results — even if you're not planning on writing an award-winning novel any time soon.

Suss out a question that you think your target audience would like answered, and answer it effectively — in an SEO-focused manner, considering keywords, metadata and everything else that has been explored in earlier chapters. Q&A pages can work if done well (and not over-done). However, ultimately, if you appropriately bring together an answer — presented in whatever format — with keywords and other SEO tactics, that's the path to real blogging success.

VIDEO KILLED THE EVERYTHING STAR

There's no doubt about it — video is huge. While some businesses might have been able to afford ignoring it for a while, it's at the point now that just about everyone is using it. According to stats from British company Wyzowl, 63 per cent of businesses surveyed were actively using video as a marketing tool in 2017, and these numbers will have only grown since then. In a local context, about 40 per cent of our clients have video on their websites in some form or another — and I expect we will see this figure grow. It makes sense, when you consider that 61 per cent of us are watching online video every day!

Video also has a crucial benefit in terms of how much attention it demands from users. While many will skim an article at best, people are more likely to actually give their full attention to a video — and therefore take something away from it. At the same time, however, we're in an era of autoplay, so you need to make sure that your video content is memorable enough to stick in someone's mind even if they've let the next five videos that YouTube or Facebook suggests play afterwards.

The dominance of video over other kinds of content does depend on the demographic in question — and so consideration of your target audience will help inform just how integral to your content plan video needs to be. Generation Z and Millennials are all about video, while Baby Boomers are slower to jump on the video bandwagon — they are often still more inclined to stick with slightly more tried-and-tested sources of information like news websites and email newsletters.

SORTING SEO FOR VIDEO

There are a few different things to take into account when you're rolling out SEO principles for your video content.

CONTEXTUALISE YOUR VIDEO

If the rest of your page is a load of junk, with all your hope pinned on the one SEO-optimised video element, you're not going to have a good time. The rest of the page is just as important — possibly more so — when it comes to ranking with search engines. So make sure that all the rest of the content on the page where you've posted your video is optimised as well as possible.

VIDEO TOP TIP

Bear in mind that Google doesn't usually pay attention to multiple videos on one page – it's the *first* one that it cares about. So if you're putting multiple videos on one page of your website, make sure that the first one is the one that can do the heavy lifting as far as impressing Google's bots goes. Otherwise, create different pages for embedding different videos.

CAPTION THIS

As video content becomes more and more prolific, people and platforms are also becoming more and more accustomed to user-friendly autoplay — which is to say, autoplaying videos that are muted so that you're not scared out of your skin by a sudden burst of noise as you scroll through your feed.

Many videos will accordingly have subtitles integrated into the video file, in the form of a paired-up video transcript. This way, viewers can immediately tell what's going on even if the sound is off — and elect whether or not to keep watching, with or without the sound. Of course, captions are also a vital part of accessibility, ensuring that users who are deaf or hard of hearing are able to enjoy and understand the video content, too.

All of those are reasons enough to include captions in your video — but there's an SEO benefit, too. By including the video transcript, you're providing the web crawlers from Google with more text to work through in order to assess relevance. An uncaptioned video is missing an opportunity, as it doesn't have any inherently identifying factors around it — Google doesn't sit and watch each and every video and take notes on its content, after all.

As well as subtitles throughout the video itself, include a transcript of the full audio underneath where your video plays, if practical. Google is, in essence, a semantic algorithm — meaning it will look for, and decipher, words. From a user perspective also, it's easier to scroll through your text for a specific part if they'd like to follow up or understand properly what you said, as opposed to finding a particular bit in the video recording. Lots of sites are already doing the text version of video content well, and relatively smoothly — consider this more as a written article you're including rather than a script per se.

PICK YOUR PLATFORM

You might have a variety of different end goals in mind when you're trying to get a video to do well in the search rankings. You may be striving to develop brand awareness and boost your thought-leadership profile — in which case YouTube is probably your best bet. You'll get in front of plenty of eyeballs, but you won't necessarily drive traffic back to your website.

If traffic to your site and new leads are your goal, then YouTube might not be the best option — though it's always there as a backup. Newer hosting platforms such as Wistia have tools in place that are a little more conducive to knocking your SEO out of the park, while allowing the video to sit on your own website without the file chewing into your bandwidth.

For example, Wistia will automatically insert SEO meta-data with the video, which as you've learned from earlier chapters is a major contributor to working your way up the rankings. Vimeo also has capacity to tweak the metadata of your videos — it just requires a little more hands-on work than Wistia's automated process.

FOCUS ON THE FOLD

There's something known as 'the fold' in web design — harking back to the days of people regularly reading physical newspapers. Imagine a newspaper folded in half as it sits on the table, waiting to be picked up and shaken out. The articles above that fold are the ones that you're going to pay attention to first.

The same thing applies to web pages, with 'the fold' in this case being the bottom of the screen, with any content below the fold requiring you to scroll down to see it. Anything of critical importance needs to be above the fold, so that you know for sure that people will see it when they first load your page, even if they don't bother to scroll any further.

So, keep your video above the fold to keep play counts up — ideally, make it the focus of the entire page, so that there's no doubt that people will find it and you can maximise that content that you've likely spent a whole lot of time and/or money on.

VIDEO TOP TIPS

» While your choice of image thumbnail doesn't have an outright effect on the ranking of your video, it has an effect on whether or not people are actually going to watch it — so it still has an important role to play. There's power in people — if there's a decent still from the video with an actual person in it, that tends to be more appealing than an array of inanimate objects. Do make sure that it's a relevant moment, though – you don't want a video on bike-repair tips to be represented by someone tying their shoes.

» As with every other part you can control, there's a great deal of SEO importance in the title and meta description of videos. Flip back to chapter 2 for the best-practice tips and tricks when it comes to developing excellent metadata materials.

INFORMING WITH INFOGRAPHICS

Infographics are the perfect way to successfully get across important information to a range of different people. Combining concise wording with visually engaging design, they are intended to be quickly and easily understandable.

Infographics are also a great way to tell a story, especially if that story incorporates a complicated concept that needs to be relayed in an accessible way to a wider audience. Visual cues are a major help for many people when it comes to retaining information — and if you want people to be remembering vital facts that are relevant to your business, every bit helps!

According to research analysis from Nielsen Norman Group, people see only an average of 20 per cent of the text on a web page when visiting it. Infographics are a solution to that once-over-lightly style of reading, by presenting the information in a format that's more easily able to be skimmed and still provide value.

Infographics are also eminently shareable content. As image

files, they are easy to post on a whole range of platforms, from Twitter and Facebook to Pinterest and Tumblr — as well as on your own website. But you do need to make sure that they are cleanly designed and easy to understand — otherwise there's no point in using them, as they'll just provide visual clutter.

OPTIMISING INFOGRAPHICS

While standard blog posts are reasonably straightforward to optimise for SEO once you know the ins and outs of keywords, metadata and headers, infographics are a little more complex. Since they are ultimately composed of images — or sometimes a single, flattened image — the words and figures involved aren't able to be crawled by Google's bots. Some background work needs to be done to allow your infographic to really pack a punch on the rankings.

Chapter 1 covered keywords in general, but you need to utilise them in a slightly different way to bring infographics and SEO together.

Using a short key phrase for the file title is the first important thing to consider — nothing like 'infographic-1.jpg', that's for sure! Instead, for example, if you have an infographic about where your sock company sources its sustainable yarn from, perhaps the file could be called 'sustainable-socks-infographic.png' — or something else with appropriately tailored keywords.

Alt text is also crucial, as I examined in chapter 2 — and, as outlined back then, it's beneficial for those using screen-reading software as well as for providing more appropriate text for Google to crawl. The alt text on your sustainable socks infographic might be 'Sustainable socks infographic including farm to factory information'.

It's also appropriate to include a H1 header above your infographic, so that it can be included in the information processed by web crawlers — as well as providing an easy introduction for actual people viewing your page. Meta descriptions are also necessary, as with any other web page — all the same principles apply for an infographic-centred web page as for a regular text-based page.

If you want to include a few other keywords and crucial information in a manner that can contribute to SEO, pull together a couple of introductory paragraphs between your H1 and the infographic itself — nothing too long, though, or you might risk pushing the infographic down 'below the fold'.

STAYING SPEEDY

In chapter 4, we looked at speed — and that's something important to consider when it comes to infographics, which can be slow to load. So, make sure you strike a balance between image quality and hefty size. Crisp quality and detail is important — but not at the expense of the ability of a page to load in a timely fashion. Sticking to PNG or GIF formats — or JPG if there's a photographic component — is your best bet for something that loads promptly while still maintaining a good-quality image. Adobe Photoshop has some brilliant compression settings that you can use to change file size when saving images for the web.

THE GOOD, THE BAD AND THE UGLY

So we've discussed a few core methods of creating content — but more important than the means of content creation is the *quality* of the content in question. But what makes good content, and what makes bad content?

First, the bad — so you know what to avoid . . .

QUALITY VS. QUANTITY

There are very few aspects of life where the mantra of quality over quantity doesn't hold true — and SEO-optimised blogging certainly isn't one of them! Sure, you don't want to let your blog languish with one post per quarter and nothing in between, but aside from maintaining a reasonable consistency of posting, high-quality content is much more preferable than tonnes of junky content strung together at a moment's notice by someone who either doesn't have the time to write blog posts or just doesn't have a knack for it.

SENSE CHECKING

Misspellings, poor font choice, badly constructed sentences . . . there are so many things you can do wrong to make an article or other piece of content hard to read. But luckily, they are also things that are easy to correct. Stick with simple fonts and make use of tools like Grammarly and online dictionaries — or good old autocorrect on word processors — and these kinds of issues should sort themselves out. Most importantly, re-read your content from start to finish, or have someone double-check it before hitting the publish button.

KEEPING IT RELEVANT

You don't want to create content that has zero bearing on your overall company operations or intentions. Likewise, you don't want to create an article in a rush after creating a super-optimised title for the piece . . . and therefore lose the faith of your new reader after they'd taken a chance on your blog for the first time after a careful Google search. Think about what you're trying to achieve and what question you're trying to answer, and stay on topic.

KEYWORD STUFFING

I've already touched on the fact that Google is smart — and getting smarter. Techniques of yore like keyword stuffing — cramming as many semi-related keywords into a page as possible, regardless of how clunky they might be — is a definite no-no these days, both from a user's reading perspective and in terms of ranking. Google and other search engines don't take too kindly to people trying to game the system like this, and your ranking may suffer accordingly.

Those are some of the real 'avoid at all costs' areas. Let's take a look instead at some of the things that your content *should* do — or should aim to do, at least.

TELL A GREAT STORY

Storytelling is at the heart of communication — even if that story is about different ways to approach a plumbing dilemma, or why insurance is important for flatters, or the ingredients that go into a gluten-free cracker. As humans, we love stories, and they can make otherwise mundane material much more memorable. So find your story and tell it in all kinds of ways — even if you need to enlist the help of a marketing or communications agency initially to help you to identify that core story.

DON'T KEYWORD STUFF, INSTEAD KEYWORD DISTRIBUTE!

We have already said 'keyword stuffing' is something you shouldn't do. So what's the alternative? It's all about aiming to write smarter by lightly working keywords into your content — but only where it makes sense! Distributing keywords — and synonyms, variants and related terms — throughout your content so that they appear at the top, middle and bottom of your article sends a strong signal to search engines that your article stays on topic and is an authority on the subject, which all helps.

BE COMPELLING AND HONEST

Facts are important, and facts articulated in a way that makes the reader want to find out more are even more important! So do what you can to draw your audience in, whether that's through a good hook in a title or an intriguing social media post that demands further attention and/or explanation.

PROVIDE VALUE

The thing with content — from a content-marketing perspective, at least — is that you want to be providing the user with something of value to them, even if it's not immediately pushing them to purchase your service or product. This can take all kinds of forms. Perhaps your sock company has an instructional infographic on darning socks that you love too much to throw away. Maybe your travel agency's blog has an article that includes a checklist of things you should remember for a trip to Fiji. Or your café has a video showing the way free-range egg farms run. Whatever the case, it's something that customers will find value in — and then hopefully, when the time comes for them to buy a new beloved pair of socks, or book a holiday escape, or arrange for Mother's Day brunch, they'll have your brand in mind.

FOCUS ON THE CUSTOMER

Ultimately, our companies are nothing without clients or customers. And if your content isn't providing something useful or interesting to your target audience, then it might as well not exist at all. Speak to your customer and show them that you understand their needs and concerns — and show them how you're the company to provide them with exactly what they need, when they need it.

JUST EAT IT

Every other week there's a new web acronym to learn. This one, however, has been around in some capacity since 2014, though not everyone will be familiar with it.

EAT stands for Expertise, Authoritativeness, Trustworthiness — three critical things to keep in mind when you're developing content, whatever form it may be taking. Let's break that down a little further.

Expertise is fairly straightforward. In order to make a good case for being a company a customer will trust and spend their hard-earned money with, you need to make sure that you come across as an expert. This doesn't always have to mean years of experience in the field, but it does mean you need to prove that you know what you're talking about and, if necessary, that you have the evidence and credentials to back it up.

Being *authoritative* is very much related to expertise — proving that you are an authority on this matter and that you have the reputation and background to support it. And *trust* continues this line of thought as well, through ensuring that you are a trustworthy source of information. Be accessible — through contact forms and NAP (name, address and phone number) details — and ensure that your website is up to date with an https address, as we covered in chapter 3.

What all of this ultimately means is that you need an author who knows what they are talking about — whether that's an expert on your business or industry, or a professional writer who knows their way around the research process.

The EAT elements are what make a high-quality page, as far as Google is concerned — and that quality will impact where you end up on the search rankings. So don't just throw the task of blog upkeep to the intern — make sure it's a task given to someone who understands the scope and gravity of the responsibility.

For Intelligent Ink, a content-creation agency that specialises in thought leadership and authority marketing, content was always going to be the cornerstone of their SEO strategy. From its belief that words matter (and have an impact), Intelligent Ink has taken a content-driven approach, and its results show the impact words can have. However, it hasn't always done this as well as it does today.

Launching near the end of the global financial crisis, and before authority marketing was much of a 'thing' here in New Zealand, the team at Intelligent Ink knew that they had work to do in terms of educating the market about the potential of content. As professional communicators, they also understood, from the get-go, the importance of making content both relevant and valuable to their audience.

Because of their focus on written communication, blogging has always been their key channel. However, in those early days – by their own admission – the agency was creating content for the sake of content. There wasn't a lot of thought behind it and, if anything, they were ticking the box because they felt as though they should be 'walking the talk'.

Applying some strategic thought has seen their search results improve.

'You can be the best writer in the world, but you can't create content that's targeted and relevant unless you take the time to stop and think about who you are talking to and what they're looking for,' explains Intelligent Ink's director Christina Wedgwood. 'You need to take the time to answer their questions. If you don't do that, you can create good content, but it's not going to be as effective.'

We've talked in this chapter about the importance of considering the specific questions your audience are asking, and using these as the basis for individual pieces of content. This has proven to work for Intelligent Ink: its best-performing blog post, by some way, was 'Why should people choose your business over your competitors?'

'We obviously struck a nerve with this one, and we have since updated this post to ensure it reflects our key messaging,' says Wedgwood. 'It's become a cornerstone piece of our content.'

Blogs that reflect core keywords also have a significant and long-lasting impact, such as one entitled 'The importance of storytelling for business', published in February 2017. Both these examples show that the pieces of content which resonate most with your audience will stand the test of time.

Intelligent Ink has also aimed for consistency. Whether weekly, fortnightly, or monthly (depending on internal resource), a steady flow of new content is always being created.

'Sharing the load among members of our team has meant that we've been able to commit to consistency as well as achieving different perspectives and voices,' explains Wedgwood.

Intelligent Ink drives its content creation from a preplanned strategic calendar, but also keeps an eye on things that are happening in the industry and wider business world, so it can leverage timely events.

'This approach helps with some of the heavy lifting and allows for extra posts. Our highest search volumes and resulting traffic to the website occur, without doubt, when we are posting weekly.'

Intelligent Ink has made very little investment in advertising and, seven years down the track, organic search remains the biggest channel by which people come to its website. Its carefully thought-through content is not only achieving high rankings for its chosen keywords, but organic search has the lowest bounce rate of all its sources of website traffic, meaning its content is getting engagement and meeting its visitors' needs.

KEEPING THINGS INTERESTING

Historically, some people may have seen SEO-optimised content and engaging content as being mutually exclusive, when nothing could be further from the truth. Well-executed SEO forces a writer to think carefully about what they are saying and why, which ultimately should result in a higher-quality end product.

Now that we are in a post-keyword-stuffing era, there are no clunky limitations on how you should be writing. You'll get much better results from a couple of thoughtfully chosen keywords carefully integrated by a capable writer.

TOP TIP

High-quality content is important, but if you do the research well, you don't need to be a professional writer for your content to have an impact.

CHAPTER SUMMARY

» Content exists in a variety of forms.

» Blog SEO optimisation is relatively straightforward once keywords and relevant page locations are understood.

» Video is the future, and there are ways to optimise it for both YouTube and Google.

» Infographics are another valuable type of content that has the potential to go viral.

» Always value quality over quantity when it comes to blogging.

» Google's perception of high-quality content is defined by EAT: Expertise, Authoritativeness, Trustworthiness.

SIX:

IT'S ALL ABOUT THE PLANNING

By now you should have a sense of what content formats will best suit your needs. Perhaps you'll also have some new avenues to explore, whether it's testing out video concepts or hiring a designer to pull together some slick new infographics.

Hopefully you're bubbling with new ideas — but there's another important step you need to take before you start charging forward. You need to develop a content calendar, which will form the cornerstone of your content strategy and ultimately see you continue to climb the search rankings (or defend your top spot!).

WHY SHOULD I BOTHER WITH A CONTENT CALENDAR?

If you know vaguely what topics you want to cover, and let's say you're pretty sure blogs are going to be your best bet, why would you bother with a content calendar? There are plenty of reasons.

For one thing, it's all about strategy. Just because a blog post or a video doesn't have as much permanence as a fully SEO-optimised homepage doesn't mean you shouldn't think about it strategically. You don't want to have someone spend hours writing blogs on a vague brief only to decide three months down the track that you want to change tack completely.

Content calendars also ensure that your content is delivered in a uniform manner. Maybe that means that your blog posts are all approximately the same word count, so readers know what they're signing up for when they open a post to read it. There could be consistency in the approach you take to headers — maybe your 'thing' is that all your subheadings are quotes from Shakespeare, or you simply commit to all blogs having one fresh header every couple of paragraphs for the ease of skim readers.

Ultimately, if nothing else, it'll help you stay organised — so rather than scrabbling at the last minute to think of something to write or even develop a video about, you'll have everything laid out ahead of schedule. There's still plenty of work to be done in creating each piece of content, but don't underestimate how much time can get sucked into racking your brain trying to think of a good idea when the pressure's on!

CONTENT CALENDAR TOP TIP

When preparing a content calendar, use Google's Keyword Planner tool to check the monthly search volumes for different keywords. This can help you choose which blogs to publish when, and which topics or terms don't have high enough search volume to justify a long blog post to be written on the subject.

CONTEMPLATE THE 'CALENDAR' ASPECT

One useful thing to remember when it comes to this part of content planning is that your calendar can align with the actual calendar — it doesn't have to be a simple Week 1, Week 2, Week 3 set-up. So utilise what's going on in the outside world to your benefit.

Planning content for your funky cartoon-sock company? Think about a fun little video for mid-October about your creepiest designs, in advance of Halloween. Or maybe even play up the idea of dads getting socks and underwear as gifts for Christmas with a blog highlighting why this happens.

Got a café with a super-popular feijoa crumble? As soon as feijoa season hits, write a fun blog post with the recipe! You're not doing yourself out of business, because plenty of people will see the mouth-watering recipe and decide that it's still much easier to come and visit you to try it, rather than risk making it from scratch themselves.

If you're a medical insurance company, maybe schedule a video on ways to avoid injuries while travelling this summer, or an infographic on winter illnesses to encourage people to take up your coverage of flu jabs.

There's always something in the real-world calendar that's influencing your business. Give it some thought, put your spin on things, and you'll have plenty to run with.

AUDIENCE OUTREACH

While your core web presence might be tailored for your one main audience, content is the place where you can play around with secondary targets or even start approaching entirely new audiences. Or, if you really do only have the one audience, it's still the way to stay fresh and interesting in their minds.

Make sure you know who those target audiences are before you launch into content planning — and create personas for those people. Even within 'one' audience there will still be variety.

Think about it — even if your core target is tradies, there's a lot of variation within that group. There will be people who are new to the field and willing to get advice on new products from anywhere, and who are very internet savvy — and then at the other end of the spectrum, but still within your target audience, there's the older folks who are approaching retirement age. They're set in their ways and would really need something incredible to shift them from their pre-existing brand loyalty . . . and they aren't necessarily computer pros.

You might already have data to use, or it might be worth doing some research before you start whipping up ideas for your perfect customers. Surveys are always a good starting point, and you can easily pull something together using a platform like SurveyMonkey or even Google Forms at a pinch — and then social media and electronic direct mail (or EDMs) are easy ways to get the survey out there. You can ask questions both about your service or product as well as getting demographic information about people, to get a sense of what kinds of people have what kinds of opinions.

Hopefully, once you've pulled together the data alongside your own understanding of your market — maybe even with a focus-group session in there somewhere — you can start to develop mini-profiles of your typical customers, to create target personas. Give them a name, and go into specifics. It might feel a bit excessive, but you never know when that detail will come in handy. As for the names, once you and your team are familiar with these personas, instead of going into a long spiel about the kinds of customers you're focusing on this month, you can simply say 'This month we're all about Brian' and they'll understand what you mean.

Here is a persona example:

Brian is 36, with a steady job in IT and a passion for new and cool gadgets. He has a girlfriend who he lives with, but no kids. He grew up on *Teenage Mutant Ninja Turtles* and *He-Man*, and his enthusiasm for those cartoons of his childhood never went away. He has strong opinions on both the prequels and sequels of the *Star Wars* franchise. He drives a perfectly decent Honda Accord, but really wants a Tesla – until they came out, he wasn't really a car man. His disposable income mostly goes on cool tech, but there's a definite window for nostalgic buys too.

And here's another:

Charlotte is 25 and fancies herself an influencer-in-the-making. She lives in Grey Lynn and studied communications, and spends her weekends scoping out the next best brunch spots. While she loves good food, in many ways her priorities are aesthetics and nutrition before taste – so she can get those beautiful shots for her Instagram and a caption that reads 'Can you BELIEVE this gorgeous spread is totally gluten-free?'. As well as her growing Insta-following, she's big on word-of-mouth recommendations.

So for Brian, your sock company might want to create a listicle-style blog post — 'Seven of our favourite weird talking animals from 90s cartoons', for example. Pull at those childish heart strings — and swing in with the links to your related socks, trying to make the socks as relevant to the article as possible.

For Charlotte (who we assume is not your prime target if you're in the sock business, but could be for your new raw food café), you want to showcase your own Instagram-worthy dishes, so she's compelled to come and see for herself. Maybe even pull together an educational but tongue-in-cheek video — the art of low-key Eggs Benedict photography.

HOW FAR IN ADVANCE SHOULD I BE PLANNING?

You probably don't want to have a piece-by-piece breakdown of content for anything more than six months in advance — too much can change in that time. You will want to work in an iterative manner so that you can build on the pieces of content that are most successful, and revise your content calendar accordingly.

As part of your plan, you'll need to establish the frequency of your different kinds of content. If your focus is purely on blogging, you'll want to ensure you've got weekly posts planned — fortnightly at the very least is preferable. But at the same time, there's no single answer. Just like when it comes to social media posts — where one 'expert' will suggest three posts a day while another 'pro' will be staunchly supportive of four posts per week — there's no magic formula.

The one thing I would suggest is that you err on the side of as much as you can handle — that way, you'll have it front-of-mind more often and will be less likely to forget about all your carefully thought-through plans. It's certainly easier to dial things back than to try to add even more to an undoubtedly already heavy workload.

You will, however, want to make sure that you've got a valuable cache of posts for people to read through, and for you to be able to link to within other blog posts — which may mean going a bit wild with lots and lots of writing at the beginning. Think of it this way: if you're a psychotherapist building your profile, you might have an article on coping with exam-time stress for high school and university students. Then, when you write an article about more serious ongoing anxiety, you can link back to the exam-stress article when identifying different kinds of stress, pressure and anxiety, providing useful related information without sending them away from your website.

For now, just make sure you're building a range of topics. You'll want to be quite specific for the first couple of months at least — then you can schedule a follow-up check-in further down the track to expand on your existing ideas and topics for the rest of the posts in your calendar.

That being said, the more you can produce up front the better — so if you've really cracked the code and find yourself at the perfect balance between caffeinated energy and creative spirit, get as much out of your brain in that moment as possible, and fill up as much of those six months as you can!

TOPIC PLOTTING

You don't have to rely purely on your own ideas and creativity to come up with topics to cover in your content. You're certainly a vital part of the process — you should know, after all, what your customers' interests or questions are — but being on the business side of the conversation might mean you don't immediately recognise all of the things that people on the customer side want to know.

Talk to your wider team — if you're in the office and they're on the frontlines, they'll have a very different perspective from you. If there are questions that retail staff are answering every day — perhaps there's a way to address that via a video, blog or graphic. That way, not only will some customers get the answer they were seeking, avoiding that particular recurring query, but you'll also ensure that your staff have the answer easily available to them.

For example, perhaps you have a bookstore and customers want to know why there's a difference in pricing between your bricks-and-mortar store in New Zealand and on platforms like Amazon. Save your staff from stumbling through an answer by giving them an easily accessible company line to use. They could even refer people to your website for further information on the topic, in beautiful infographic form.

If you don't personally run your social media, talk to the people who do. Again, you'll get a sense of what questions are being asked, what posts are most popular, what kinds of demographics are engaging with your content — all valuable information to further grow your plan. You can even delve a little deeper and investigate forums and chat rooms focused on the topic relevant to your industry. Check out Reddit for heaps of super-niche communities that could relate to what you're trying to sell — you might identify topic possibilities or content ideas that haven't explicitly been raised to you before.

KEYWORDS . . . OF COURSE!

It would be a misplaced miracle if there were a chapter in a book about SEO that didn't mention keywords. Take the topics you're wanting to cover and do some keyword research so that you've got at least one or two great long-tail phrases to cleverly incorporate into your content — whether it's the intro paragraph or header of a blog post, or in the captions of a video, or even the alt text of an infographic. I don't need to go into too much detail here, since we've covered keywords at length already.

You want to focus on the customer experience here. If there's a topic you really want to cover, that you really think is valuable but that doesn't necessarily have the same powerful keyword search terms, don't second-guess yourself. Other posts that are more keyword-oriented can pull people into your blog, and your important content can shine in the sidebar — or be the focus of a killer series of social media posts.

THE QUESTION OF LENGTH

Long form is great – but not at the expense of quality. You don't want to try to build a blog post on a small (but great) idea and force yourself to arbitrarily hit 2000 words.

Three hundred words is the bare minimum for a blog post to be able to rank on Google. Data compiled by CoSchedule noted that the average blog is 1142 words long. The trends are moving from shorter to longer, with multiple studies suggesting that

2500-word blog posts rank best. However, that doesn't take into account what actual people prefer to *read*.

The same data suggests that if you're looking for comments on the post, something as short as 275 words is best – which stands to reason, if you think about the fact that people will usually need to read all the way through to the bottom of an article to get to the comment box. Unless they have a very strong opinion right at the beginning and immediately scroll all the way to the bottom, they need to actually have the time to read – or at least skim – the article. For shareability on social media, on the other hand, the most success was seen on posts with between 600 and 1500 words.

So take your goals into account when contemplating length – but don't bolster your word count at the expense of quality of work.

CASE STUDY: BRINGING IT ALL TOGETHER FOR TEAM SOCK-IT

Here is an example that pulls together some of the main points – using our famous sock company as our go-to. These guys are onto it, so content is an important part of Team Sock-it's digital strategy. They understand that regularly posting fresh blog content serves the double purpose of providing an SEO benefit and increasing engagement with website visitors.

They've undertaken research to find content opportunities for the following six months – based on strategic keyword research, search trend and competitor analysis – and put together a content calendar outlining proposed topics for March through to August.

First, here is a list of Team Sock-it's target keywords:

- » Socks
- » Pop culture socks
- » Cartoon socks
- » Made in NZ socks
- » Sustainable socks
- » Pop culture accessories
- » Pop culture apparel
- » Cartoon accessories
- » Cartoon apparel
- » Anime socks
- » Manga socks
- » Animation socks
- » Fun socks
- » Gift socks
- » Nerdy socks
- » Nerdy gifts
- » Trendy socks

And here are their proposed blog topics:

MONTH	PROPOSED TITLE	INTERNAL LINKING KEYWORDS	SUMMARY
March	A history of socks	Nerdy socks, sustainable socks	When did people start wearing socks, and what materials were they made from? When did they start becoming fashion statements? This blog will speak to the fact-focused among the 'nerdy' pop culture fans, as well as exploring the sustainable material used to create Team Sock-it socks, within the framing of a timeline of different materials.
	Which socks suit your style?	Trendy socks	Some people like an anklet sock with their favourite cartoon character hidden away. Others wear their geek pride loud and proud and in full colour. Can cover different cuts of sock as well as styles – large loud print versus more discreet pattern. Can then link through to appropriate socks for each recommendation.

MONTH	PROPOSED TITLE	INTERNAL LINKING KEYWORDS	SUMMARY
April	Michelangelo, Leonardo, Raphael and Donatello – masters of paint and pizza	Cartoon socks, cartoon apparel, cartoon accessories	The Teenage Mutant Ninja Turtles experienced a resurgence in interest with a new movie in recent times – but there's nothing like the original. But what does each turtle have to do with their Renaissance namesake? A tongue-in-cheek look at classic artists and these cartoon heroes.
	Where can I wear my Team Sock-it socks?	Socks, pop culture socks	A visual and written account of where people have worn their Team Sock-it socks – whether at high-powered business meetings or on holiday overseas or in hospital to bring some colour and joy to a long stay.
May	Five features of top-of-the-line socks	Socks, made in NZ socks	Focus on the design features and processes that make these socks top quality, with behind-the-scenes video content.
	How to darn your best-loved socks	Socks, sustainable socks	DIY video and transcript instructions. Focus obviously on the hardiness of these socks, but also highlighting the fact that they are so awesome you'll want to wear them until they are totally threadbare – and this is how to give them a second wind.

MONTH	PROPOSED TITLE	INTERNAL LINKING KEYWORDS	SUMMARY
June	Winter sock recommendations	Socks, gift socks	It's winter in the southern hemisphere, so here's a feature of the best winter-weight socks that Team Sock-it has to offer. Add a small section at the end on lightweight socks for those lucky enough to be escaping winter to somewhere summery.
	Queens of the Kawaii socks	Anime socks, manga socks	Focus on the range of different anime and manga that are popular locally, across a variety of genres (drama, comedy, etc). Bring attention to iconic symbols and characters that feature in sock designs – and even play off sock trends in the shows themselves (e.g. the best white knee socks for your cosplay needs).
July	The world's greatest sock puppet tutorial	Socks, fun socks	Sometimes, socks are destined for a second life as performers on the smallest stage. A tongue-in-cheek tutorial on making awesome sock puppets and putting on the performance of a sock's lifetime – with video content and images.

MONTH	PROPOSED TITLE	INTERNAL LINKING KEYWORDS	SUMMARY
	Paging Captain Planet	Cartoon socks, sustainable socks	A feature on this particular cartoon character in parallel with a feature on sustainable practices within Team Sock-it – both in production of the socks and with any corporate social responsibility programmes that are in place.
August	Stepping out for the occasion	Socks, pop culture apparel	There's more to Team Sock-it than simple ankle socks. Explore different fashion statements and ensembles with examples from the Team Sock-it collection, including tights for cold weather, leg warmers for a twist on slouchy socks and any new/different products (hats, scarves?).
	The best Father's Day socks money can buy	Socks, gift socks	With Father's Day around the corner at the start of September, get ahead with your planning and order a pair of the funniest and coolest cartoon socks for your Dad this year. Socks are traditional – but they don't have to be boring!

CHAPTER SUMMARY

» Yes, you do need to create a content calendar
– to keep you organised, if nothing else.

» Tailor your content to the time of
year and real-world events.

» Contemplate your target audiences – both your main
core and secondary audiences – and personalise them.

» Establish a planning timeframe.

» Plot out your topics and remember to use keywords.

» Think about the best length for your blog posts,
for SEO and also for the user experience.

SEVEN:
HOMETOWN ADVANTAGE

The internet may open you up to the whole world, but unless you're an online retailer with great international shipping capability, chances are high that your core customer audience is people in your part of the world — possibly down to your city, suburb or even neighbourhood.

The good news is that the current state of the web means that you can make use of specific SEO tools and techniques in order to rise in the rankings when it comes to local search. But how local is local? It depends on the area your business or brand services, which could range from national, country-level marketing to the city you're in or the geographical area (even suburb!) around your store. Either way, this chapter will start with the wider view and then tighten its radius.

CASTING THE NET WIDER: INTERNATIONAL SEO

Let's start by assuming you are one of those aforementioned businesses with great international shipping capability, for whom the world is your oyster. If this is you, chances are you'll want to consider what is commonly termed 'international SEO'— the process of optimising your website so that search engines can easily identify the countries you want to target and the languages you use when you do business.

International SEO becomes important if you know you have lots of visitors to your website who come from a different country to the one that you're located in — or who possibly speak different languages. And as well as making sure they have the best possible experience of visiting your site, international SEO practices will ensure that you specifically target traffic from further afield.

First, you may want to consider an international-friendly URL structure, which starts with a country code top-level domain (ccTLD). It is likely that your current website has a .co.nz or .com.au ccTLD, which indicates to both users and search engines the country which your website is targeting. If there is another country — say, across the ditch or further afield — that you want to attract significant traffic from, you might set up a website with another ccTLD. Although this can be expensive to maintain, it gives the clearest geographical-related signal to search engines, so it's the easiest way to rank locally. Bear in mind, however, that employing this method means that each site will have its own domain authority (e.g. .co.nz and .com.au), so you'll have to apply your SEO efforts to each website in their entirety.

Another temptation, as it's easier to maintain than additional ccTLDs, is to put your internationalised content on a subdomain — a separate 'third-level domain' such as 'http://country.yourwebsite.com'. The problem with this, however, is that each subdomain is also still treated as a completely different website by Google, and therefore can't harness all the link equity (the result of all your link building) as effectively and pass it between the sites. For example, your New Zealand website might get a lot of inbound links from other websites and then perform well in search engine results, but the Australian website won't be able to leverage all this link equity because Google sees it as a separate website with no inbound links. You will need to do all the SEO work for each region separately — including the link building.

As you can see, operating individual websites or subdomains is a lot of work as everything multiplies — from search console registration and diagnostics to link building, blog/content creation, audits and more. There is an easier and more efficient option: create what are referred to as subdirectories (or subfolders) with 'hreflang' tags. This is code that indicates to search engines which countries and/or languages your site wants to target. An example of this would be:

http://yourwebsite.com/en-nz
– in English for New Zealand users

http://yourwebsite.com/en-au
– in English for Australian users

This can be difficult to implement on some sites and may require developer intervention, but it has multiple benefits:

» One website/CMS is easier to maintain.

» There will be much better user experience overall, as the user can switch between countries and be served that content.

» Content creation and uploading can be streamlined – no more creating blogs for each individual web domain.

» Link equity (which you'll learn more about in chapter 12) will flow between the sites seamlessly. For example, if your Australian site gets a lot of publicity and inbound links, the New Zealand website will also benefit from it.

» It solves the important duplicate content issue with Google. If you have the same or similar content for both websites – such as products or services with only pricing and currency differences in different regions – with hreflang implemented, Google will understand that both pages are about the same topic, and produced by you, but meant for different regions – and this will therefore not hurt your rankings.

When it comes to international SEO, there are many other things you should consider, such as creating content that's suited to your target audience, in their local language. Using their dialect, colloquialisms (if you choose), currency, time zone and local contact information sends strong (and important) signals to both Google and users that they're in the right spot. You might even want to consider how your brand is presented, and the overall design of your site, to take into account any cultural differences.

BEYOND ENGLISH

If you are wanting to go beyond English, here are a few best-practice things to remember:

» Make sure that everything – from your content to your site's navigation and support function – is in the primary language you are targeting.

» Localise – don't just translate. Get proper translations done by a human being who knows the culture instead of doing a straight word-for-word translation. Different objects, colours and terms have different meanings around the globe.

» Use geographic redirects to improve the user experience. If a user from France goes directly to the US version of a website, you can ask them if they'd prefer to go to the French website instead, based on their IP address. Either way, don't make assumptions.

Lastly, it can help to have a local server in the geographic region that you're targeting. Alternatively, you might want to investigate the use of a 'content delivery network' or CDN. Put simply, a CDN is a system or network of distributed servers that can serve up web pages to a user based on their geographic location, the origin of the web page and the content delivery server used. This can help with SEO, as it improves the time it takes your website to load and improves the user experience — both of which we know Google views favourably.

If you're not an international retailer, some of this will have less focus — although you'll likely have a country code domain and local inbound and outbound links, by default. But just because you won't be sharpening your tools further from an international SEO perspective, that doesn't mean there isn't much you can be doing to benefit search-wise, based on your geography. In fact, it's even possible to do local SEO at a suburb level.

Given the majority of Kiwi and Aussie businesses still do business within their country's boundaries, the rest of this chapter will focus on optimising for a 'hyperlocal' strategy that focuses on the relevance, proximity and prominence pillars to search. We'll explore tools and techniques to help with this, the first of which is Google My Business.

GOOGLE MY BUSINESS

Sure, it may sound like a command, but Google My Business is a specific Google tool that can help businesses and organisations really stand out across various Google platforms — not just in organic search rankings, but other areas such as the 'Maps Pack' or 'Snack Pack' of Google's results and in Google Maps.

A verification process ensures you are who you say you are or, at the very least, that you're operating out of the address that you tell Google you are. Once verified, your business is officially claimed by you, as far as Google is concerned. That means that you'll be able to adjust the information that shows up when people are searching for your company — or for the sorts of services or products that you provide.

HOW DO I CLAIM AND VERIFY MY LISTING?

Just because your company now appears in the right spot on Google Maps doesn't mean that you can automatically start tinkering with the details. And similarly, if you don't show up on Google Maps, you also cannot just dive right on into things and craft a listing from scratch without Google validating what you're claiming.

Before you can do any editing, you need to claim your listing — and there are two different ways that you can do that. First, check to see whether or not you already have a Google My Business listing. Head to google.com/business and hit the 'Start Now' button — helpfully peppered throughout the page.

You'll be prompted to enter the name of your business. If Google's already aware of the company, it should pop up for you to select. If you're new to the tech giant, you'll be able to hit the 'Create a business with this name' button, then follow the prompts to fill in the relevant details in order to start creating your listing. This process is easy, but you really do need to make sure that your listing does not already exist, as having a duplicate listing can cause many issues down the line.

Next is the actual verification, where you have two options. You can opt to get a code sent via automated message to your business's phone number or, alternatively, you can arrange to have a postcard with a code sent to your business address. Both get you to the same end goal — but, needless to say, calling is naturally much faster than waiting for 'snail mail' to arrive.

Once you have that code, log in to Google My Business and there should be a Verify My Location option in the menu. Select that, enter your code, and you're good to go.

DEALING WITH DETAIL

The aim here is to keep Google happy, and to provide as much relevant information for potential customers or clients as possible. Getting that information front and centre is crucial when you're trying to sway someone in your direction rather than towards one of your competitors.

Why is all this stuff important? Let me give you an example. Maybe your business is a café in Sandringham, and you haven't loaded your hours onto Google. You're closed on Mondays, but open every other day and, what's more, you're open late — a rare thing indeed in most Kiwi cities! You've put your hours on Facebook and on your website — but you've neglected to give this information directly to Google.

Here's two potential scenarios:

Someone comes across a gorgeous photo of your smashed avocado on toast on their friend's Instagram, and they decide that they absolutely have to look you up and go visit. They Google you. They find your address. They set out, looking forward to a brunch treat . . . on a Monday.

They arrive to your shut door and are disappointed. Oops. You might not get them back.

Or perhaps someone is looking for a spot for a late-afternoon/evening catch-up with a friend, but would prefer to do it in a café rather than a bar. You're the perfect fit, right? But while they are flicking through different 'Sandringham café' results, if you don't actually state that you're open late, will they find you? Or will they just give up and settle for the local pub instead?

The moral of the story is that supplying all the information that will impact your potential new customers' decision-making is absolutely crucial. So carefully go through and make sure that your hours, your phone number, your address, your appointment-booking link, etc are all present and correct . . .

All of this important information needs to be watertight.

THE CATEGORY IS . . .

To be certain that you get the right search results, you also need to make sure that your primary category is appropriate. You don't want to find out weeks from now that local searchers haven't been finding you because you were not tagged in the right category. You can tag your organisation under up to 10 categories if they are relevant to what you do.

You won't always find a category that precisely aligns with your offerings, and unfortunately you can't create a new category just to suit your needs. However, if you look a little more generally, you'll usually come across something appropriate. If you're really lost, have a quick look at what your competitors have listed themselves as and use that as a launching point.

TOP TIP FOR BUSINESSES WITH DELIVERY

For some businesses, it doesn't matter where your customers come from, as long as they know where you are. So if you're a café or a boutique that doesn't deliver, you can disregard this point. But if you're a service provider, or a retailer or hospitality business that offers delivery, it's wise to indicate a delivery radius.

In the Address section of your Google My Business listing (under Info in the menu), there's an Edit button. If you click this, a window will appear that asks whether or not you are a delivery-based business. If you do things at a bricks-and-mortar location as well as via delivery, that's fine, too – just make sure you check the box that says 'I also serve customers at my business address'.

You'll have the chance to set your area in a couple of different ways – either by selecting the postal codes and/or the cities and towns covered (if you've got a regional or national reach). Or for something a little more simple, you can select a radius in kilometres around your location.

PICTURE THIS . . .

I've mentioned earlier the value of photos in the context of ensuring they are tagged appropriately. When it comes to Google My Business listings, things are more straightforward — the pictures are the star of the show.

The profile picture itself is the most critical thing to get right. It'll receive the most impressions of all the images you include, so it needs to do a top job of representing your business. But do put careful consideration into the other images that you upload too — be sure to paint as thorough a picture of your company as possible. Don't just snap a couple of photos on your phone and call it a day — make sure that you're creating the appropriate vibe for your company, whether that's slick and professional, fun and creative, or trendy and modern.

If you're a boutique retailer, showcase your shopfront and your product inside. Think about including photos of the shop with people browsing, even if it's a staged set-up. Spaces come to life when people are in them, and you don't want to risk people overlooking your business just because it doesn't look as welcoming as others.

The same sort of rules apply to restaurants and cafés — make sure you get someone confident at food photography to take some standout shots of your star dishes. Service provider? If your service is able to be photographed, do it! Maybe you're a moving company — think about a picture of a carefully packed truck and a photo of a couple of cheerful-looking staff carrying boxes. More of an office-based business — maybe an accountant, or law firm? Stick to high-quality photos of the interior and exterior of your office space so that you can convey the right sense of professionalism.

But if you really are short on time or photography budget, exterior shots of your business premises may be your best bet — they'll have the right branding, and they'll also be a visual aid for people when they are tracking you down while walking or driving down your road.

KEYWORDS ARE STILL KEY

Whether someone is typing 'dentists in Kilbirnie' or simply searching 'pizza near me' while their GPS is letting Google know they're in central Nelson, having the right location-related keywords in the right places is vital.

Your title and meta descriptions can pack in those crucial snippets – for example:

The Tooth Fairies – Kilbirnie's Dental Experts
We provide the best in patient care for the young and old.

A relaxing environment with convenient hours, we think we're Kilbirnie's best dental practice – and you will too.

The best pizza in Nelson | Bebe's Pizzeria
Get the most authentic and most delicious pizza in Nelson at Bebe's. Expect nothing but the best of fresh ingredients and good vibes.

THE WORLD IN REVIEW

As users of the internet, we have all made decisions based on reviews by others. Whether a review encourages us to do something — a 4.8-star restaurant would catch anyone's eye — or persuades us not to — a 2.1 out of 5 stars company isn't one you likely want to give your business to — it's an integral part of that decision-making process.

On Google, these reviews are arguably even more important than on any other platform. This is because your rating isn't just impacting people's decision-making habits, it's playing a role in your organic Google search ranking.

There's strength in numbers, so encourage your current and past customers to write a review for you on Google. Maybe include a link to the review page on emailed receipts, or include a small reminder (nothing too over-the-top) in a regular email newsletter. If someone's written a nice comment on your Facebook or Instagram, reply thanking them, and suggest that they could perhaps write a quick review on Google 'so that more people can have the same great experience you did'.

Of course, in addition to making those kinds of requests for comments on other platforms, it's important to respond to reviews on Google, too. Thank people for kind reviews, personalising the content wherever possible.

> Thanks for the feedback, Chad, we're so glad you had a good time! The mushroom risotto is one of our favourites too. Can't wait to see you next time.

> Hi Katya, we really appreciate you taking the time to write your review. I'll be sure to send on your thanks to Barbara – she'll be delighted to hear you had such a successful night.

In an ideal world, all your reviews would be glowing. However, sometimes we have to face up to less-than-enthusiastic feedback. Keep things professional and thoughtful — and if there's a situation that can still be fixed, do what you can to make that happen. A customer who feels heard and understood is much more likely to give you another go — and maybe change their tune.

> Hi Bianca, I'm so sorry to hear about your experience – we pride ourselves on trying to always provide the best service, and unreservedly apologise for letting standards slip the day you visited. If you email feedback@yourwebsite.com, I'll organise a refund, or alternatively we'd be happy to provide you and a friend with a free lunch if you're willing to give us another go!

> Our apologies, Bob – we agree, that's not good enough. I've passed on your feedback to our management team, and someone will be in touch directly with you later today to resolve the situation.

RECENT ADDITIONS TO GMB

One of the 2018 additions to Google My Business was the Q&A feature — a highly valuable tool for businesses and consumers. Potential customers can ask questions — for example, if your restaurant has a vegan option, or if you have any Mandarin speakers at your financial advisory firm — and get answers right from the horse's mouth.

You also have the benefit of seeing what kinds of questions people are asking — and be able to assess whether or not you could be providing that information more prominently somewhere else. If you're a boutique kids' clothing company and someone asks you if you stock children's clothing . . . you clearly aren't getting your brand across!

Just like you'll need to keep tabs on the Google My Business listing in case of errant edits, you'll also want to pay attention to questions as they appear — unanswered questions aren't a good look, so be sure to stay on top of things. You can download the Google Maps app and use that to respond to questions as they appear. It's all part of enriching your listing, both for humans browsing things and Google ranking things!

Some other new Google My Business features are:

» the ability to add the date when a location was opened

» a 750-word description of your business

» a menu or services list for your visitors to look at

» the ability to create a 'business site' – a single-page website that you can generate from GMB. Make sure that you link this business site back to your main website.

KEEPING YOUR GMB LOCATION LISTING UP TO DATE WITH GOOGLE POSTS

To promote something that's less vital to your profile permanently, but relevant for a short period of time, Google Posts are a great solution — and a great way to further nudge that ranking upwards. You can create content around events, products and services, and it'll directly show up on both Google Search and Google Maps.

Maybe you have a new product arriving in store, or a sale coming up. Perhaps there's an event on the horizon or an exciting change in the leadership of your business. You can create your Google Post, using 100–300 words and enriching things with imagery — and even a call-to-action button if appropriate. Is 300 words enough to get the message across? Add a 'Learn more' or 'Book now' button that can link through to a page or blog post on your website for more information.

This functionality can be accessed through the Posts option on the menu to the left when you're in your Google My Business account. Each post will be live for seven days after posting, so take that window of time into account when you're planning your supercharged posts.

MAP THE PATH AHEAD

When it comes to coming out on top on Google Maps listings, most of the factors at play are covered off in this chapter, as there's a lot of interplay between Google Maps and Google My Business. One little extra move you can make is to embed a Google Map on your website's contact page.

To ensure you get the most out of this addition, make sure that your NAP (name, address and phone number) information is consistent across your website, any online directories and your Google My Business listing – otherwise Google is going to be confused about why your business isn't where you said it was.

BEYOND GMB

It's easy to get caught up in Google My Business when thinking about how to be impactful in the local space. But once you've perfected your listing and drafted up some posts in advance, as well as setting a reminder to check your questions and reviews, there are other things you can be doing back on your own website to work towards better capturing the local market. While your Google My Business listing should probably be your first priority when it comes to cracking the local SEO code, it's important to consider other avenues too. Yelp, Zomato, Neighbourly, Ranker, Yellow Pages and a range of other industry and local directories are very helpful to get citations, mentions and back links from.

You can carry over a lot of the same information that you pulled together for your Google My Business listing — in fact, it's probably worth saving those details on a spreadsheet or other document to ensure that everything is consistent across the board. And on that same document, make sure you've got a list of all the different sites with listings, so that when it comes time to update something, you know all the places you will have to make those changes.

It's important to keep tabs on the review aspects of these and other platforms, too. Take the same approach of professionalism and personalisation in your responses, regardless of where the review has been placed. You never know — someone who has posted something unkind on a relatively obscure review site might decide to broaden their audience with a tirade on your Google My Business listing at some point.

SCHEMING WITH SCHEMA.ORG

Schema.org was introduced in chapter 3 – that useful extra data you can integrate into your search listing across Google, Bing, Yahoo! and Yandex. Various pieces of schema data can be relevant to local businesses, from opening hours, to types of payment accepted, to events, to maps . . . There's a lot of potential, and the schema.org website contains a library of all the different options.

CHAPTER SUMMARY

» An accurate and well-maintained Google My Business listing is a crucial part of local businesses ranking well both on Google and Google Maps.

» Go all out on details and photographic representation – this is your chance to sell yourself!

» Prove yourselves to be an accessible, customer-focused business through thoughtful review responses and answers to questions.

» Consider the local implications of your keywords and Schema.org data.

EIGHT:
THINKING BIG

Companies can have big reputations — but all too often, they also have big blind spots. For many corporations and enterprises, SEO can seem unnecessary, or get relegated to the 'nice to have' pile rather than the 'must do' pile.

But take a look at a calendar. We're nearly in 2020, and companies that elect to continue to ignore cornerstone parts of digital marketing could ultimately do so at their peril. It's a rare company that doesn't have a growth agenda of some kind, and if you want to continue to grow and develop, rather than stagnate, harnessing the power of SEO is critical — even if you're a well-known organisation.

Think about it. If you aren't developing SEO tactics but your competitors are, who are new customers — who are inevitably relying heavily on Google when making decisions — going to stumble across? Sure, your name might be a familiar one to them, but if you don't come up on the first page of Google when potential customers are typing in search terms relevant to your industry, you're toast.

It's all well and good to say that SEO is an essential part of corporate marketing in this day and age, but it's a whole other thing to actually instigate change in this space. Corporations are, by the nature of their size and scope, slow moving — and often slow to take to new ideas. So in this chapter, I'm focusing on how SEO can be different for large corporate entities — with some suggestions on how you can go about overhauling your SEO at a basic level.

STARTING FROM SOMEWHERE SLOW

I mentioned above the slow-moving tendency of corporate organisations — and that can affect all the different parts of the business. It can take a long time to implement institutional-level change — a decision made on new hardware or approval for something as simple as a blog post can be a long and arduous process.

The result can be websites that stagnate. Unless someone managerial in the content space has the implicit trust of the top of the food chain and is able to make general moves and updates without a massive amount of box-ticking, there's going to be . . . well, a massive amount of box-ticking. Knowing that there's a drawn-out process for getting content approved and uploaded can make updating websites a lower priority, especially if news is no longer new by the time it makes it to your front page.

Sometimes, you might not be able to change those processes — it might be a fact of life if you're simply part of the Australasian arm of a multinational entity. But if you do have access to people with some kind of sway, make the most of that. Do your research — pull info and figures from places like this book and make your case for why SEO is an integral part of a modern marketing approach.

Whether or not you do have the power to make waves and change processes, there are still things that you can focus on, if you're part of the marketing team. It may not be as transformative as if you were able to go all in with a full audit and change plan, but it can still help you work towards pulling things in the right direction — especially if your website already carries decent domain authority.

CASE STUDY: CREATING CORPORATE CHANGE AT KORDIA

Jennifer Johnson is the Group Marketing Manager of Kordia, a state-owned enterprise that provides mission-critical technology solutions to a wide range of businesses throughout Australasia. As a corporate entity, they have some rather different challenges than those faced by smaller companies – and those differences extend to their SEO needs.

'Within the Kordia group there are a number of companies in one, with numerous internal and external stakeholders. Kordia runs a very busy calendar of marketing activity in-house, and for our SEO needs we needed a partner that had the right level of expertise and technical understanding. We chose to partner with Pure SEO to ensure our core websites were getting the attention they deserved,' Jennifer says.

In a large organisation like Kordia, there are frequently new services and offerings being developed, requiring new keywords and content to be developed. The situation is ever-evolving.

Kordia recently had two new websites created, representing separate brands and businesses: one for the main Kordia business unit at kordia.co.nz, and one for its independent cyber consultancy, Aura Information Security, aurainfosec.com. But while they had been well designed, there was room for added expertise in search engine optimisation.

'Initially we conducted an independent audit and hygiene check, focusing on the H1 tags and the structural layout. From there we started to look more generally at each site to see how pages are performing,' Jennifer says.

'Following on from the initial audit and recommendations, we've had great success with a fortnightly WIP [work in progress] meeting, with reporting that allows us to pick out what needs to be focused on and what needs to be brought up to speed.'

The new websites mean the team has faced a challenge in terms of what data they have to work with, but now that the new approach has been in place for over a year, they are starting to gather the appropriate data points for decision-making and assessment. And it has paid off, with their organic search traffic certainly growing.

An important element of working in the corporate space is understanding the challenges that you're dealing with. 'It's an ongoing process of developing that understanding. We operate in a complex business with various moving parts,' Jennifer says.

'We also run a very heavy calendar of content, and we're able to use a lot of that in the SEO space. It helps build our credibility.'

Jennifer also says you need to get into the detail to fully understand the complexities of SEO.

'I think it highlights just what a minefield it is, how it requires such a detailed focus. It's one of those things where people just think you tick a few boxes and you're set. But Google's forever-changing algorithms mean you need to partner with the right business and maintain a consistent focus on SEO.'

If a new website is being developed for your organisation, try to put in your two cents at the front end of the process. It's going to be easier (and more economical!) to handle web-content changes at the same time as web-design changes — and it's certainly going to make more sense to develop that content on the basis of good SEO practice rather than adjust content to fit SEO needs further down the track. Again, bring the facts and figures with you to the party to back up the case for proper SEO — and underline the fact that things will be a whole lot simpler if these things are considered from the outset, before coding starts.

If you're handling your company's SEO needs yourself, or you're the single conduit between your company and your SEO service provider, you can rely on simple reporting methods that are focused on what you are aiming to get from the process. (Chapter 15, which tackles metrics and measurement, should steer you in the right direction.)

However, if you're part of a large corporation, you may well find yourself needing to provide different information to different people or departments.

SEO specialists can help to develop automated reporting processes that suit the different departments who have their fingers in the pie. You can provide insights for IT teams as far as straight-up technical SEO issues go, with more high-level performance metrics for management teams.

If there are marketing business partners for different units of the business — for example, if you're a civil engineering company with different groups for transportation engineering versus structural engineering — then you can provide insights to those marketing specialists as to what is working or not working within that line of the business. The breakdown can be as detailed or as broad spectrum as your business requires.

It's also important to maintain open communication between any SEO specialists and the teams affected — rather than relying purely on reporting and letting the numbers speak for themselves, make sure that conversations and explanations take place. You want to always provide context.

LITTLE THINGS FOR BIG BUSINESSES

So you're part of the Auckland branch of the New Zealand arm of the Australasian division of the Asia-Pacific sector of a massive international company. The person who uploads content to the company website isn't even in the same time zone as you, let alone the people who approve that content. And yet you're in the business of marketing. How can you work within your strict constraints while still pushing your company forwards in the digital space?

If you're involved in writing blog posts, consider all of the things that I've covered in the previous chapters on keywords and content. As long as you're sticking to your style guide and toeing the company line, working your writing around keywords should be a no-brainer. Be sure to make note of where you have integrated those keywords though, so that a) they don't get subbed out in an editorial process, and b) those doing the checks and balances have their attention drawn to the fact that you're taking this into consideration.

A powerful content strategy can make a big difference, especially if you're then internally linking to that content from other blog posts and pages. In terms of social media, if you don't have easy access to company social accounts, share from your own LinkedIn account, and encourage colleagues to do the same. You might get some shares from friends in powerful places, which can only help your cause!

But you also must remember that, just like the fact that the decision-making process takes time, so too will results. When you're already a vast company, the time required to see substantial growth in organic traffic could be considerable. Make it clear to those you report to that this is the case: that while this shift in digital focus is important and will have an impact, that impact won't necessarily be immediately visible.

Ultimately, the main difference for a corporate entity compared to a SME is the ability to leverage your brand's existing reputation and marketing — along with its links, visibility and relationships. It's also about trying to be as nimble and flexible as your competition.

CHAPTER SUMMARY

» Corporate needs are on a different scale to SMEs in all areas – and SEO is no different.

» There are different ways you can start to make changes in SEO practice, regardless of how hands-on you are able to be with your company's website and online channels.

» Time is needed for change to happen – and it's also needed for external digital marketing providers to understand the ins and outs of a corporate company.

» Don't be afraid to make your voice heard when it comes to supporting change for the better in the search space. Harnessing search is an inevitable avenue for all businesses in this day and age, so help your company be ahead of the curve rather than chasing after it.

NINE:
LET'S GET ENGAGED

The first thing to mention in this chapter is that digital engagement is a specialisation all of its own. People could — and do! — write whole books on topics that I'll cover here, like conversion funnels, landing-page design and calls to action. And it's not strictly part of SEO, though there's a great deal of overlap between the two areas.

In particular, there's a great deal of connection between on-page SEO activities and aspects such as landing pages and call-to-action buttons, as they all tie in to making sure that the bones of your website are as good as they can be.

This chapter will provide you with basic guidance to kick-start your digital engagement tactics.

WHAT IS ENGAGEMENT?

Digital engagement can mean different things to different people, at least in terms of execution. But in sweeping terms, digital engagement focuses on digital methods of engaging with customers, or potential customers. It's that simple.

Done well, it can be the start of a conversation that leads to an ongoing relationship or a conversion. Done poorly, it can deter people from dealing with your business in the future.

Techniques to create engagement can take many forms. There can be markedly different approaches depending on whether you're selling to an individual representing a business's interests (B2B — business-to-business) or to an individual representing their own personal interests (B2C — business-to-consumer).

CREATING CONVERSIONS – FIND YOUR FUNNEL

In rugby, you convert a try to get more points. In digital marketing, you convert a visitor into a customer. Both kinds of conversions are part of a winning strategy. The way to make conversions happen is to have a stellar conversion funnel in place, to carry people to the point of decision-making.

There are many different parts to a conversion funnel. Organic search is one major factor — no need to delve further into explaining that right now. Social media also plays a crucial role these days. And beyond that, external content and online communities can play their part. PR falls into the funnel. Referral links on other websites, email campaigns, advertising across search, display and social media — and even good old word of mouth all add together to create this funnel.

Think about surveys you might have filled out for businesses in the past — invariably, there will have been a question along the lines of 'where did you hear about us?' Basically, any answer to that question is an entry point of the conversion funnel.

A funnel, by its very nature, narrows as it reaches the

bottom. A conversion funnel is no different. Realistically, you have the most customers at the point of entry — when they first come across you and your business's website through one of the mediums mentioned. Whether they clicked on a link in a tweet or looked you up after hearing about a friend's good experience, they are part of the broad 'acquire' phase of the conversion funnel.

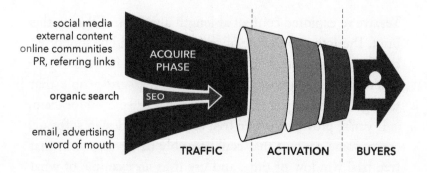

The idea behind the conversion funnel

ACTIVATE YOUR AUDIENCE

After you've scooped people into your marketing funnel, from various parts of the internet and the real world, the next goal is activation.

What activation looks like for you will depend on what your business creates or produces. You've got people on-to your website — maybe you've even got them to sign up for an e-newsletter, or to follow your social media account. Activating them is the part of the process where those leads turn into buyers.

If you have a software product, this could mean offering a 14-day free trial. If you're a service provider, it could be a free consultation. If you're selling groovy socks, it could mean a 50 per cent discount on your first purchase when you use a special offer code. It's all about something that will spark interest and get people to take the next step.

CONTENT CONTINUES TO BE KING

Yes, we've explored content at length already, so I'll keep this brief. The activation phase of conversion should be supported by great content that relates to the offering in question — where possible, anyway. You want to reassure people that taking this first step is a fabulous idea that will pay off for them.

If you're providing a free trial of a piece of design software, create some content that could feasibly be developed in that free trial window of time, and use it as an example of what people could achieve with limited time and rudimentary understanding of the program. If you're providing a free hair-colour consultation, let people know what they can expect the consultation to include — maybe develop a cheap and cheerful video with a stylist discussing the sorts of questions they'll ask, and then a few shots of some beautifully coloured hair. If you're our famous sock company, why not gamify things and put the onus of social media marketing on your customers-to-be:

> Use the code sockittome at checkout for 50% off your first order – then post a pic of you and your new Team Sock-it gears in the wild with the hashtag #teamsockitnewrecruit and you'll go into our monthly draw to win a $100 Team Sock-it gift voucher!

BECOMING BUYERS

If you've succeeded at activation, you'll hopefully have a crop of real customers just around the corner. Nobody likes a pushy sales pitch — so make sure that any interaction with customers in the activation phase is persuasive without being unbearable. If you're offering a free consultation, for example, talk up the benefits and the way you do things differently.

Emphasise that you understand that the customer needs to know they're making the right decision — but ideally make that point once you're already fairly confident that you've got them on side. You're not going to win every time — and that's OK. Nobody has a 100 per cent conversion rate — in fact, most websites convert less than 2 per cent of their total traffic.

This is the part where proving that you understand your customers' needs is vital. There's no point trying to push for bulk-buy discounts for orders over $1000 if you're selling socks directly to consumers. There's no point trying to sell an enhancing (rather than critical) software system to small businesses if there's a large retainer fee. Demonstrate that you know their drivers or challenges, and how you're going to fix them. You want to show authority without arrogance, and really push your value proposition to make sure that customers understand how you're going to make their lives easier or better — or both.

It doesn't matter what kind of product or service you're selling. Cartoon socks to cockroach bombs, hair styling to panel beating — ultimately you're there to make people's lives better in some way, right?

THE THREE RS

Reading, wRiting and aRithmetic, right? Sure, when you're in primary school. But when you're playing in the big leagues of digital marketing, the three Rs that you need to commit to memory at this point are Retention, Referral and Revenue.

You've made a sale, got a booking or otherwise made a good enough impression for a customer to part with money (or at least their credit card details) in exchange for something that you're providing. Excellent.

But you don't want to have to restart this whole process all over again every time. Restart may start with R but it's not a word we want to focus on, that's for sure. Instead, retention is the name of the game.

How do you retain customers on an ongoing basis, or ensure that they are repeat customers if your product is more of a once-in-a-while purchase? There are more options than you can shake a stick at, and what works for one company won't necessarily work for another. But here are a few things you can keep in mind when trying to straddle the delicate boundary between being lacklustre and being pushy — finding that perfect moment of encouragement.

TAILOR YOUR APPROACH

We've already looked at the need to consider different buyer personas (see chapter 6). This can apply equally to post-sales communications as it does to appealing to those at the top of the conversion funnel. And it's even easier at this point, because you'll have relevant data to work with. If they've purchased a pair of socks that you can identify as being in women's sizes and related to a particular fandom, you can push them into a specific avenue of retention-related communications.

Perhaps you have the same basic email, but slightly different versions in terms of the imagery used and the testimonial snippets you include. It's a little extra work, but think about how much more likely you are to buy a product again if you're getting reminders that speak to your own interests.

Maybe your customer is Violet, 28, interested in retro pin-up fashion and cute prints, and she purchased a pair of socks with sailor-style swallows on the ankles. You could send her a generic email, with a testimonial from Chad, 42, who loves his new Space Jam socks. Or you could send her an email with the same general information, but a testimonial from 31-year-old Tracey, who is gushing over her new tights with a vintage Barbie print. Which one do you think is going to speak to Violet's interests more?

WORD TRAVELS

Referrals are the dream. A customer who tells someone else about your company in excited, enthusiastic terms is going to be more effective than even the best online ad campaign — you just can't buy that kind of magic.

But in order to get people referring, you need to make sure that the process you have in place is excellent. The last thing you need is for someone to compliment a customer on their socks and then have them reply that they bought them from you but you were a pain to deal with.

Easier said than done, of course — but if you have a quality product and a suitable purchasing process in place, then you're setting the groundwork for people to feel positive about both the experience and end result. And with a bit of luck, they'll shout it from the rooftops. This is another of those spots where the magic of social media can come into play, with an offer of freebies when people tag you in posts or use a specified hashtag.

A PLACE FOR ARRIVAL

Your landing page is essentially the page on which visitors to your website first arrive — or 'land'. More to the point, it's the page that you direct people to arrive or convert on. For example, you may have a particular landing page for a specific advertisement set on Google Ads, and another landing page for people coming through from a Facebook advertising campaign.

You may think that it's simpler to just direct people to your homepage — and yes, that would be simpler. But it wouldn't be as *effective* — both for the visitor and for you. Landing pages allow you to speak to the needs that have driven the customer to click that specific link, rather than assuming that your homepage can do all the talking and explaining for you. It also allows you to focus on one specific call to action — more on that in a moment.

SMOOTHING OUT THE LANDING

Landing pages shouldn't be complicated — but they do require some thought and consideration. You want to pack a punch with the content, hitting all the core points so that people feel informed enough to follow through with whatever call to action you've incorporated — without overloading them with information.

A good landing page should allow a seamless transition through to the activation phase of the conversion funnel.

People have been interested enough to click — make them interested enough to take the next step and book or buy.

LANDING PAGE TOP TIP

A/B testing can be a good way to make sure you're headed in the right direction with your landing pages. It's a simple enough concept that most advertising platforms will allow you to play with. You can create two (or more) iterations of the same landing page, and provide the links to both of them in the one ad. Google Ads or whatever service you're using will randomise the pages, and you can track which ones see the most success in terms of conversions.

CALLING OUT FOR MORE

In the context of a landing page or other digital marketing avenues, a call to action or CTA usually takes the form of a big shiny button, ready for potential customers to take them to the next stage of their customer journey, whatever that may be.

The easiest and most effective options are things that may seem obvious but do a good job: 'Call us now', 'Click to book a consultation with us', 'Sign up for our newsletter', 'Subscribe now', 'Get started'. Give your customer immediacy through slightly urgent wording, and a sense of entering into a community of actual people by using terms like 'us' and 'our'.

As far as where you should be putting the button, different people will tell you different things. An immediate reaction might be to keep it above the fold so that it's obvious — right there ready to be clicked. And for some companies, that might suit. However, research from MECLABS actually demonstrated a 220 per cent higher number of leads from a longer landing page (with the CTA button at the bottom) than from an equivalent page with the button before the fold.

Again, it depends on what you're selling, and how you're selling it. If it's something that's a big investment or otherwise requires a great deal of customer trust, more information that makes a case for you as a reliable business is going to be a key part of getting that all-important click on the button.

Wherever you put it, make sure it looks good — and on brand. It's a major sales tool, so you want to give it the attention it deserves. Prove your value through your landing-page material — and then clinch the next step with a CTA button that is slick, professional and tempting.

CRO (CONVERSION RATE OPTIMISATION) TOP TIPS

» Create urgency with the user, pushing them to book or make a purchase. For example, if you are a hotel or tour operator, use language such as 'Only one room left!' or 'Free for a limited time!'

» Make the call-to-action buttons such as the 'Book Now' or 'Start Your Free Trial' buttons more salient on the page as well, by using a colour not replicated anywhere else on the site so that the buttons instantly attract a visitor's eye.

» Pages that are designed to convert users are more successful if they include 'social proof' such as user reviews or testimonials.

» If you have an e-commerce website, and a user abandons their online shopping cart with items in it, you can set up your content management system to automatically send out an email 15 minutes later, asking them if they want to complete the transaction with a 10% discount.

ENGAGEMENT TOP TIP

Remember, the best initial engagement strategy in the world won't have ongoing power if you have a dud product to sell. You might get plenty of acquisition, and even a great deal of activation – but for that all-important repeat business through retention and referral, you won't get the ongoing feed of revenue. A smaller number of carefully captured loyal customers is much more valuable than a vast wave of one-time shoppers who won't have anything good to say further down the line.

CHAPTER SUMMARY

» Engage your customers throughout their journey with you for optimum results. Digital engagement is not technically SEO, but it can play nicely with it.

» Conversion funnels are all about scooping up a large number of people at the top – there is always some inevitable drop-off.

» Activate your potential customers with exciting offers and tempting opportunities where they can get to know you and your product.

» Create effective, efficient landing pages with considered CTA buttons to help on the final stretch of bringing those potential customers home.

TEN:

THE ERA OF USER INTENT - RANKBRAIN

As you've discovered in the previous chapters, SEO has seen many advances over the years. While you don't need to become a specialist in all these aspects to do SEO well, you do need some level of understanding of how they work. One such development is the move towards machine learning to power and process search results. Witness a recent Google search innovation — RankBrain.

Artificial intelligence (AI) and machine learning have taken the world by storm over the past decade or so. We're starting to see the application of AI in a range of different everyday applications, from online customer support, chatbots and virtual personal assistants to smart home devices or music and movie recommendation services such as Spotify, Pandora and Netflix.

Essentially, AI is about getting computers to respond to situations in the same way that humans would. It's about introducing elements like judgement, perception, reaction and decision-making — all factors that, until recently, didn't exist in computers. Machine learning is a type of AI that focuses on experience — in much the same way that we learn and improve over time, based on our memories, a computer will remember the outcome of a previous situation, and adjust its reaction accordingly.

These two concepts are critical to RankBrain. RankBrain seeks to understand what a user is looking for (using AI), then improves the experience each time based on previous searches (machine learning). But before you start picturing robots well and truly taking over the world — and your mind — let's take a look at how RankBrain actually works.

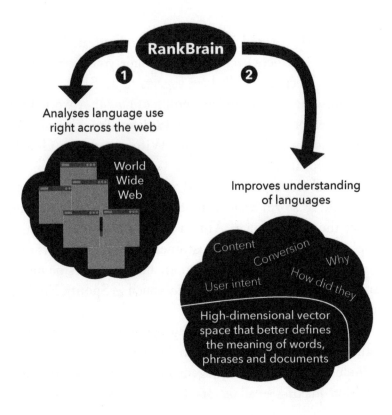

UNDERSTANDING HOW RANKBRAIN WORKS

RankBrain looks at a user's *intent* when searching — inferring the meaning behind the actual words they use in a search. It then customises its user experience, and the results it serves up, based on that. Basically, RankBrain is related to the processing and refining of search queries. At first it used pattern recognition to tackle complex or ambiguous search queries and connect them to specific topics and content, and now it does this with all search queries.

Put another way, RankBrain's algorithm is geared towards understanding user intent, linking this to common searches, and presenting these results. RankBrain teaches itself to sort through the billions of web pages online and return the results in terms of relevance, which we can all agree makes for a better search experience.

More amazingly, because of its machine-learning component, RankBrain teaches itself over time — making ever-smarter connections between search terms and desired results, so since its rollout in early 2015 it's improved its understanding. In 2015, RankBrain was used for less than 15 per cent of queries. However, since that testing by Google — and as confidence in its results has grown — RankBrain is now used in the processing of every query that Google handles.

Because RankBrain is continuously learning from its original programming as well as developing new connections, it allows Google to be proactive — making assumptions about what you may be searching for, based on the words you use and your previous behaviours.

Let's consider an example . . . say you search 'best bar in Auckland'. What you're likely to want to see is articles and listicles comparing the top bars in the city. You want lots of information, so you can read through and do your own comparisons, based on what 'best' actually means to you. What you *don't* want to see is a bunch of websites claiming that they have the best bar in Auckland — that's not helpful to you. If you search 'best bar in Auckland' and only get ads or articles about specific bars, you'll probably do another search — something like 'top 10 bars in Auckland' — which will hopefully then show the results you're after. RankBrain's job is to predict this in advance and understand your intent based on your initial search, linking this to other, more common searches, and presenting you with those results.

It's not a whole new way of searching, but instead an addition to Google's overall algorithm that includes other ranking factors focused on fighting spam, improving local results, favouring mobile-friendly sites and demoting ad-heavy pages (among other things!).

RankBrain differs from previous search engine practices in its interpretation of search terms. Think of it as a 'query interpretation model'. Basically, it's aiming to return results that are related to, but do not necessarily contain the same exact words as, the original search. It also focuses on effectively interpreting 'long-tail' queries to find the user's intent. As you might imagine, RankBrain is also improving the way that Google understands the different meanings that one word can have, applying an understanding of context to avoid irrelevant results.

WHY DOES RANKBRAIN MATTER?

Google processes three billion searches per day and estimates suggest that 15 per cent of those are queries that it has never seen before; that is over 450 million totally new and unique queries every day! Among those are 'long-tail' queries (complex, multi-word searches, like when you type a whole question into Google). RankBrain effectively translates them, seeing patterns and connections or similarities between different complex searches, in order to determine what relates to particular topics and to find the best pages to serve up in its results.

As we've already seen, Google's mission (like any business) is to ensure the best experience of its users — which in its case means providing the best results to searchers. RankBrain is key to this; it exists to provide Google users with the search results they want to see. Because of this vital role, RankBrain has rapidly become one of the most important factors in search engine marketing. In fact, Google itself recently announced that it was the third most important factor in determining search rankings, behind quality content, which we explored in chapters 5 and 6, and links, which are explored in chapter 12.

This is good news for searchers who can't always come up with the keywords that they need, but also has implications for anyone wanting to make the most of search marketing for their business.

The introduction of AI means that Google's algorithm is even less straightforward to explain than previously. That said, in some ways RankBrain furthers our understanding of how search environments are changing. The feedback loop that's leveraged by the frequent measurement of results means that it's possible to continuously improve SEO copywriting and more easily understand the impact that changes to a website have on its ranking, which is ultimately good news too!

CAN YOU OPTIMISE FOR RANKBRAIN?

Most of the experts agree that there is no way to optimise for RankBrain, in the strictest sense of the term. You might be wondering why you're here, then — or why I've included a chapter about RankBrain in a book to help you DIY your own SEO, but bear with me.

Unlike some other ranking signals, like page speed or mobile-friendliness, RankBrain doesn't assign your website, or web page, a score that determines its position. Instead, RankBrain helps Google to determine which signals it should prioritise within its algorithm, based on its interpretation of user intent. And as such, it requires a different type of thinking — which is great for those who aren't technical SEO experts.

It would simply be too much to outline here all of the ranking signals that Google's algorithm takes into account as it determines what results appear on a Google search page, and how they are ranked; there are — literally — hundreds. However, Rand Fishkin's example, used for one of his famous 'Whiteboard Friday' instructional videos, helps with understanding how this works in a very real way. (For more of these entertaining vlogs, check out https://moz.com/blog/category/whiteboard-friday)

Let's say you're looking for ideas for what you should be

watching on Netflix. You might type any of the following queries into Google:

best Netflix shows

best shows on Netflix

what are good Netflix shows?

good Netflix shows

what to watch on Netflix

And the list goes on . . .

Whichever way you look at it, these searches are all essentially asking the same thing. Despite the fact that they use different words and phrasing, RankBrain helps Google to understand that they should all be answered with the same (or at least the same kind of) content. Having established user intent (you're wanting a list of the most popular shows/movies on Netflix), Google uses RankBrain to basically say, 'now what signals are right for me to enhance or to push down for these particular queries?'. In this way it determines the priority of these other signals or factors.

Considering the Netflix example further, RankBrain might determine that in the case of this particular search query, links from a vast range of sources are not that important here, but freshness (how recent the content is) is extremely important. This is logical as, if you're doing this search, you're expecting up-to-date results. No matter how many links are pointing to that article, it's unlikely that you want to see what the best shows were in 2015, especially if some of that content may no longer be accessible on Netflix — so Google will downplay the link diversity signal and enhance the influence of the freshness or recency.

SO, HOW DOES UNDERSTANDING RANKBRAIN HELP YOU WIN?

While there's no definitive or strictly technical way to optimise for Google's RankBrain, there are ways to achieve subtle positive shifts. The good news, too, is that the thinking required to achieve these mostly just requires us to apply some good old human common sense. As I've mentioned, it's about creating content more naturally, and employing fewer of the other SEO 'tricks'. RankBrain may be a highly complex machine-learning algorithm but at the end of the day, it's not rocket science — and us humans are smarter. So let's take a look at what works — and what really doesn't! — when it comes to SEO in this new era of RankBrain.

THE NEED FOR A HUMAN MIND

Regardless of the rise of AI programmes, it is still humans (and not bots!) who are using search engines. We're searching in a more fluid and conversational manner than ever before, and this will only amplify as we see an increase in voice search in the coming years. It is vital to be able to see your website, and your blog content, in the way that users will see them, and not just based on what you think Google will like. Choosing keywords, writing content and optimising web pages with colloquial language focused on intent has become the new normal.

Gone are the days of trying to get inside the mind of an algorithm or system. RankBrain exists to provide the best content for people, so the best way to leverage its benefits is also to focus on people. Most users are not SEO experts, so they'll click on the links most relevant to what they are looking for.

Static, automatic approaches to SEO won't work here, so you do need to roll your sleeves up and play the role that only humans can. Think about your visitors' behaviour, and what changes or improvements you can make to your site or content to provide a more enjoyable user experience.

TAKING KEYWORD RESEARCH FURTHER

We saw in chapter 1 how vitally important keywords are, and how they become the foundation for all things SEO. RankBrain doesn't change that; you should definitely still focus on keywords, but you should also dive deeper, and take that research a little further. We need to look beyond generic keywords for the precise search engine queries that your customers will be making.

Consider the intent behind your keywords — what are users actually wanting when they search for 'best bars in Auckland' or 'marketing in New Zealand'? The easiest way to do this 'behind the scenes' work is to simply put yourself in the user's shoes. If you were looking to find great marketing firms in New Zealand, what would you enter into Google? And what would you expect to see in the results?

Ask other people about how they search and build those insights into your thinking; you may be surprised to find that different people (and especially those of different generations) will search for the same sort of thing in a very different way — despite their similar intentions.

Constantly run your keywords through this experience-based lens and use this to inform your content planning. In the age of RankBrain, those who don't make this adjustment, and instead just continue targeting keywords and common search phrases, will be left behind.

TOP TIP

Google can also help, as it gives handy hints down the bottom of the page with its 'related searches' list. This is another clue that helps you think beyond just the search terms that people specifically type in.

CAST YOUR CONTENT NET WIDER

You'll know from the previous chapters that content is still king — and plays a vital role when it comes to SEO. This overarching rule still applies in the age of RankBrain. So, what do you need to consider in terms of content, as far as RankBrain is concerned?

The key point here is the increased importance of generating more *inclusive* content. If you want to rank well for something, it's critical to cover all aspects of a topic and answer as many questions as possible about it. As well as keeping real-life people in mind when planning and creating content, strive to be as useful, helpful and inclusive as possible.

For example, building on our 'marketing in New Zealand' example, you might create content that looks at how marketing has changed in New Zealand, what's important for marketers right now, your take on some of the great marketing campaigns currently happening or ones that you think are exhibiting 'best practice', and top tips for people trying to choose a marketing agency or partner.

Ultimately, if you aim to provide information which is in-depth and useful for your audience, then you share the same goal as RankBrain, and will be well on your way to winning.

TOP TIP

Look around! It's not the best idea in all arenas, but in search land it pays to act like everyone else if you want to rank for a particular term. Analyse the top competing pages and see what they have in common with each other that you could implement (with your take on it!). That said, be careful not to plagiarise.

When it comes to actually creating your content, keep your searchers' intentions firmly in mind. Once you understand what users are really meaning when they search for a term, you can use this as a platform for generating great content that will rank highly and drive traffic.

RankBrain means that content creation is now about writing to the fringes. By that, I mean that rather than targeting one specific keyword or phrase, it's about including a range of synonyms and variations, as well as other words that might commonly occur in the same sentences. This makes it easier to generate more natural content, as you're not trying to get one term or keyword in there as many times as possible (which, I can tell you, does not tend to make for a good read — plus users are savvy enough to notice, and tune out, when they see this!).

All of the other principles for writing good content still apply, but here it's key to also remember that your user is a person — quite possibly in a hurry — who is looking for your product or service. They will search for the first thing that comes to their mind surrounding the need you fulfil and, for different consumers, this will be different words. Write in a broad enough way to cover as many of these options as you realistically can, and your content will be better positioned to succeed.

Also remember that not every searcher is ready to buy something straight away, so create content that caters to wherever they are in their decision-making cycle. Considering the previous example: if you understand that users searching 'marketing in New Zealand' are looking for information around marketing practices, and are not wanting to be sold marketing services immediately, you can then write educational pieces around this subject, like those wider content suggestions made previously. Considering content in this way will help you to generate potential leads for your business who will, ultimately, be much more open to buying from you at a later time.

WORD VECTORS

If you want to get more technical, RankBrain relies on similar principles to those of 'word2vec', an open-source program that utilises a large body of text to visually represent word associations. Basically, word vectors refer to the way that words and phrases can be mathematically connected. Essentially, word2vec counts the distance between words and phrases, then presents a diagram showing how related each word is to another. Google has a word2vec tool that enables you to play with your own machine-learning project if you want a greater idea of how it all works, at https://code.google.com/archive/p/word2vec/

CHAPTER SUMMARY

» RankBrain uses artificial intelligence and machine learning to interpret search queries and determine a user's intent in order to rank results in terms of relevance.

» There is no specific way to optimise for RankBrain, but some of the overarching rules for good SEO, especially those around content, still apply.

» RankBrain is attempting to think like a human, so apply this thinking (and lashings of common sense!) to your website and content generation.

PART 2: OFF-PAGE SEO

ELEVEN:
AN INTEGRATED APPROACH

This chapter — and this second part of the book — takes us down a slightly different path. Now that you've developed a more well-rounded understanding of on-page SEO, it's time to look at off-page SEO . . . and beyond that, at some aspects of marketing your business that aren't even focused on SEO.

Yes, this book is about SEO — that's why you're reading it. But just as I discussed how it would be foolhardy to think that SEO starts and stops at identifying keywords, it would be foolhardy to assume you can maximise your business's potential through working some back-end SEO magic alone.

Even digital marketing companies whose bread and butter is developing and implementing SEO strategies for companies know that there are other avenues to pursue. That's why this chapter has a case study focusing on my company, Pure SEO, and how we have made a combined approach work for us.

It's also important to note the 'integrated' part of integrated marketing. It's not just multiple different areas of marketing operating side by side — it's different areas of marketing that are all singing from the same song sheet. Unified messaging with tweaks according to platform is going to make a lot more sense to a consumer than seeing all kinds of different approaches from one company. And it's going to save you time, money and effort if you cunningly repurpose material when it's feasible to do so!

At Pure SEO, obviously we know very intimately the power of great search marketing, but we also appreciate the fact that it's not the be-all and end-all from a marketing perspective. That's why we've tried most things — from branded vehicles and signage, to PR, through sponsorship and speaking at events, to radio advertising and Google Ads — to get the word out and grow our brand and business.

They say that someone needs to see your brand at least three times before they will engage with it, and I firmly believe that to be the case. The more people experience our brand, both on- and offline, the more likely they are to convert. Or, put another way, the greater our brand recognition, the more comfortable prospects get with the idea of us and the more likely they are to interact and, ultimately, buy. I've also found that those who engage with us after several different interactions — for example, they've read a few blogs and perhaps signed up to our emails — tend to stick with us as clients for longer than those who convert immediately, say from a single display ad. So what does this mean from a search perspective?

The value of off-page activity from an SEO perspective tends not to be immediate; in fact, it's hard to measure return on investment (ROI) immediately. But, just as positive brand recognition is accumulative, so too are the benefits from search — they're ongoing, like the 'gift that keeps on giving'. Much like building a business, succeeding at search marketing requires doing plenty of hard yards at the start before you begin to reap the rewards. There's no such thing as an overnight success, but it's worth it when you achieve those great rankings as, once you're there, it's harder to be displaced (although maintenance is still important!).

At the end of the day, search engine optimisation is part of your overall marketing mix; it's not a miracle panacea. Yes, search is incredibly important — people are searching on Google, so you need to be seen there — but it also has its limitations. Search alone is unlikely to turn your business into a rocketship; you've got to do other things too.

BRAND RECOGNITION

Brand recognition is cumulative. In many cases, it's about the small steps that all add up to have a big impact over time. That's certainly the case with search. And as this chapter — and this part of the book overall — illustrates, marketing activity doesn't operate in silos — all the off-page stuff comes together to provide search value in various ways.

PR activity and media mentions bring with them citations and links, increases in website traffic and the value of having your brand written about, even when a link is not being created. For humans it's about brand awareness and positioning, and for Google, it's all credibility and popularity votes.

PR & SEO

PR often falls under brand awareness. This area is covered at greater length in chapter 14 — where I look at both PR and influencer marketing — but it's worthy of mention here to underscore the fact that it's part of the broader marketing piece. PR is a distinctly separate skill set from general marketing, but if harnessed properly it can be a major enhancer of a successful SEO strategy.

They may seem incredibly different on the surface but ultimately, both SEO and PR hinge on messaging. A successful PR campaign can drill a specific key phrase into a consumer's head, which then influences their future searching habits. And when a well-executed SEO strategy pushes your company to the top of the search page for that key phrase, your company will still be in the consumer's mind courtesy of the PR campaign, making a potential customer more likely to hit your link instead of someone else's.

IT ALL ADDS UP

One of the most valuable things we've done from a marketing perspective (and also one of the most enjoyable!) was a trip I took to visit Richard Branson at his private retreat on Necker Island in the Caribbean, following an invitation through Entrepreneurs Organization (EO). The off-page potential was huge: the resulting PR generated us links from top-tier media. From an article in *The New Zealand Herald* alone we signed six new clients. From this, one could claim that PR is more effective than search in this instance, but that's not the whole story — and, in fact, we take a far more pragmatic approach to our marketing.

As a business, search sits within our marketing mix and is subject to the same testing, tracking and metrics. We measure everything in terms of business impact and return on investment. We analyse and report on all of our marketing activity on a monthly basis so we can see the things that provide an immediate return, as well as understand those that don't. And that's where search comes in.

Some kinds of marketing are designed to be punchy, in your face, and immediate in their effect. SEO is not one of those areas. By bringing together other methods of marketing with SEO, which steadily drives along in the background, growing and developing day by day as long as you've created the right environment for it, you'll create a much more comprehensive marketing plan and find that you're covered now and later.

SPIN-OFF BENEFIT: MASTERING THE ELEVATOR PITCH

Once you've condensed your business down to some vital key phrases through developing your SEO strategy and content, constructing really effective and cutting elevator pitches is going to be a great deal easier!

PAID ONLINE OPPORTUNITIES

Sometimes, in order to get the ball rolling in a rapid and powerful way and really make sure that people are paying attention to what you have to say, you have to pay for the pleasure. There are plenty of traditional avenues to do this, and many of them are incredibly expensive — think billboard campaigns and television or radio campaigns. These are often effective, but painful as far as upfront cost goes.

However, if you have some spending power — just not enough for a primetime TV slot or a Queen Street billboard — there are multiple different online avenues available to you, which could prove just as effective for your needs. With a level head and careful planning, you'll definitely get more bang for your buck.

ADVANCING WITH GOOGLE ADS

If you've got the cash for it, Google Ads can be a company's best friend. And the fact that Google is in its name is probably indicator enough that it's a great avenue to take in your expansion beyond organic SEO. Using Ads doesn't actively enhance your organic search ranking, but it plays a part in visibility and building trust. If your company shows up at the top of Google's results page in an ad, and then a few spaces further down in an organic listing, you're getting double the exposure that you would with just the organic result — and you're going to stick more clearly in people's memory.

Google Ads is also an amazing resource when it comes to tapping into the best possible keywords. The Google Ads Keyword Planner Tool — don't say that five times fast — is the best tool around for researching the keywords for SEO. And its super-straightforward to use this particular tool, too — all you have to do is enter a few basic keywords that you're already aware of, and it will generate screeds and screeds of relevant keywords, with all the ranking and power information you could ask for. Your research doesn't have to be only on the generating keywords end of things, either — you can also check to see if the keywords you've already selected are going to have a good conversion rate.

The one thing to consider, however, is that aside from the nice and easy keyword tool, Google Ads isn't really a beginner's game — it takes a little while to wrap your head around everything, and when you're ponying up money for the service, you want to be as efficient as possible as quickly as possible. So this is an area to either a) outsource, b) hire an in-house specialist, or c) ensure that you or whoever is going to be running the Google Ads campaigns is appropriately upskilled before kicking things off. You don't want to watch money go down the drain while you muddle your way through.

THE WIDER PPC UNIVERSE

Google Ads isn't the only option when it comes to paid advertising online on a PPC (pay per click) basis. If you're a B2B (business-to-business) entity in particular, LinkedIn's advertising platform can be incredibly useful, especially given the level of targeting available. If you have a product you want to target to HR practitioners, you can target it to HR practitioners. If you provide a corporate office-cleaning service in Hamilton, you can target it to people who work for corporates in Hamilton.

There's also the option of sponsored updates, which are useful if you have a particularly eloquent writer or comms specialist on your team, whose posts already do well but could do even better with a bit of spend thrown behind them.

Facebook also offers PPC advertising, and that may be a good option if your target audience is more general consumers. There's a whole host of different variables and options that you can play with, including integrating advertising for Instagram, allowing you to appear in people's timelines and feeds alongside the posts from those they follow. Ever wondered why you see ads that seem curiously well targeted to you? It's because the person who created the ad knew what they were doing, and ticked all the right boxes.

For example, perhaps the targeting is designed for an overlapping section of folks who have interacted with pages that have to do with 90s anime, but also who have liked a specialist garment page. Team Sock-it fits into that niche, and the people viewing the ad are much more likely to be curious about the product.

With any of these PPC options — whether Google Ads, Facebook or LinkedIn, you'll be well served by your existing SEO work, because you'll know exactly what points you want to get across with your wording in order to capture the audience appropriately.

WARNING: BEWARE OF SO-CALLED 'JACK OF ALL TRADES'

Lots of people say they can do everything from a marketing perspective, but most can't. It can pay to team up with a collection of separate specialists – ones who understand their roles within the integrated marketing mix and play well together – to maximise your performance in each of these key areas.

A good clue is to have a look at a company's own meta titles. If they're not written in a search-optimised way, it's unlikely they know what they're doing sufficiently in the SEO sphere (especially as this is such a fundamental aspect of SEO 101).

We've already covered off content in a broad way, so the basic nuts and bolts of content marketing through blogging and other avenues don't need to be covered in detail here — but once again, don't underestimate its power! There's a reason why so many businesses are hiring content-marketing managers these days, and why so many firms are popping up that offer it as a service. It's a specialised skill set, as with any major aspect of marketing. But it's also nice and easy to integrate with SEO, as I've illustrated. Keywords and writing go hand in hand.

That being said, the content that we've covered has been content in the online sense — and when you're taking an integrated approach to your marketing, it's worth considering how offline content can also play a role. Perhaps it's a paid editorial advertisement in an industry magazine, where you tell your company's story in classic print media — you could even repurpose an infographic that you've utilised in an online context. Graphically interesting learning opportunities aren't limited to screens! Maybe it's even a regular column, where you provide your thought-leadership perspective on broader topics — but always with a byline that has your name, your company name and your website address. If you play into the trends and topics of the day, the magazine or newspaper's readers may keep your perspectives in mind when they next read or hear about the topic in question. This keeps you front of mind, even if the topics you examine aren't directly related to your company's offerings.

Remember, the marketing world is expansive, both online and in the world beyond the screen. So pay attention to what that world is doing, and find ways to make your company's voice be heard everywhere — in a way that complements your SEO tactics and techniques.

CHAPTER SUMMARY

» There's more to successful marketing than just amazing SEO, even for digital marketing companies!

» Brand recognition is a core part of any business's success, and offline exposure of your brand is a core part of that.

» SEO is a slow-burn activity – combine it with other, more fast-paced marketing approaches for a well-rounded strategy.

» Paid advertising can create some quick wins, and platforms like Google Ads provide useful tools for your SEO too.

» Content exists beyond the screen and can provide valuable chances for your name and company name to linger in people's minds.

TWELVE:

LINK ACQUISITION: AN ONLINE POPULARITY CONTEST

It might seem on the surface that the only link that really matters in SEO is the link that shows up on a search engine results page — that's what all your hard work building up your SEO is aiming for, right? That carefully crafted website that means that Google ranks you highly and encourages people to click on your link through to your website, rather than any other results that might come up.

But as it turns out, other links have a lot more power than you may think. In fact, according to the latest search-ranking factors compiled by digital experts Moz, link-related features claim the first and second spots on the list of most influential ranking factors. That's higher even than keyword and content-based elements.

THE POWER OF THE LINK

Say you're a new company, with a new website. You've done your due diligence when it comes to the keyword side of SEO, with carefully considered keywords and phrases integrated in all of the appropriate places. Your meta titles are perfect, you've integrated keywords into your image alt text. Basically, you feel like you've cracked the code.

But all that this proves to Google is that you know how to handle keywords properly. That's certainly vitally important — but it doesn't actually provide any validation as to whether or not your company is reputable in any way, or whether or not you're even a real company at all.

And that's where links come in — specifically back links, also known as inbound links. If another website links to your site, it shows that your website is worthy in some way. Georgi Todorov, founder of digital marketing education site Digital-Novas, maintains that links and great content are the most important ranking factors for Google. To further make his point, he often shares this graph from Brian Dean of SEO and link-building consultants Backlinko. Tordorov says: 'It clearly shows that sites ranking number one have links from nearly 300 domains, whereas sites ranking at the bottom of that first page, in spot number 10, might have links from only around 50 domains.'

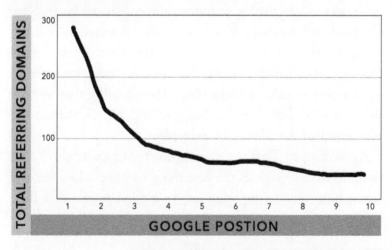

But this isn't a free pass to pay a whole lot of spammy, scammy websites to include links to your website in order to bolster your profile. As I've mentioned time and time again, Google is smart. If all of the links to your site come from places with names like freelinkbuilda.tv or buildlinks.cc, Google is going to notice — and it's not going to like it.

So you want to aim for quality companies with respectable websites — specifically, websites with a high domain authority.

UNDERSTANDING DOMAIN AUTHORITY

Domain authority is ultimately what it says on the tin — the authority or credibility that a particular domain has with Google. It's all about how important and relevant a website is related to its particular topic or field.

You can use tools like the seoreviewtools.com website authority checker to see where a specific site stands. A scale between 0 and 100 is used, according to a system developed by the team at SEO software company Moz. The tool shows you the authority of a specific page, as well as the domain as a whole.

Thanks to geography, websites from organisations in New Zealand and Australia won't necessarily manage to pull the same numbers as those in the US. But that doesn't mean that you shouldn't be taking the domain authority score of local websites into consideration. There's still going to be a difference in a link from Joe Bloggs's blog and a link from the University of Auckland, for example.

According to Todorov, the authority (or credibility) of a domain with Google is the first thing he checks in a website when he's considering whether it's a good source of a link.

However, he also warns that there are lots of so-called 'dropped domains' that people buy and fill with content then sell links from, which will — sooner or later — be penalised by Google. Often you can trust your gut on whether something is legit, but before considering where to seek your link love — by contributing a guest post, for example — Todorov recommends a few extra checks.

'Look at whether they rank well in search engines and whether any of their latest posts show up in searches. Then try to get a feel for the levels of engagement the website receives. You can also check the website's social media pages to see what sort of audience and engagement they have.'

FIRST PORTS OF CALL ON YOUR LINKING JOURNEY

The first things to knuckle down on when it comes to getting a head-start on your links are things you can develop yourself — think directory listings and social media profiles. Websites such as Facebook, Twitter, Google My Business and LinkedIn are huge, and used by every organisation under the sun — and, accordingly, boast a domain authority score of 100. Be sure to harness the power of these sites to bring up your own ranking.

It doesn't take long to create a profile on these websites — and much of the information required will be the same from site to site. Pull together a spreadsheet or document with the vital bits of information — things like your business's phone number, email address, opening hours, address, industry categories, etc — in order to have all the necessary content in one place.

The key ones I'd recommend hitting are:

GOOGLE MY BUSINESS

I've covered this at length already in chapter 7, but it never hurts to be reminded!

FACEBOOK

Facebook can prove a brilliant tool for reaching your audience — its own figures say 2.9 million Kiwis have active accounts. But you'll want to either make sure you're prepared to provide regular content updates and monitoring — or, if you're not quite ready to put in ongoing time to social media, make sure that's clear. Go into the settings and disable messaging, so that people aren't trying to get into contact with you and getting exasperated that you aren't responding.

You may want to put something about your approach to Facebook in your 'About' section, and/or in a post — something along the lines of 'We're not hugely active on Facebook, but to stay up-to-date on what Team Sock-it is up to, visit our website or sign up to our newsletter. If you've got any queries, get in touch with us via higuys@teamsockit.co.'

LINKEDIN

This seems like a fairly obvious recommendation, but one that many people neglect to sort out. When you put your new job on your LinkedIn profile — to much fanfare, of course — people will be keen to find out more about your company. And while they could, in theory, type your company name into Google, they are much more likely to take the easy route to information — in this case, that's clicking on the company name on your profile. So you want to make sure that the page they're taken to when clicking has more information than just 'Team Sock-it has 2 employees on LinkedIn'.

There should be a small 'Business Services' link in the right-hand column of your LinkedIn homepage — and when you click that, one of the options that springs up will be 'Create a Company Page'. Easy-peasy.

LinkedIn is also a place where you can make use of blog content, through the LinkedIn articles feature, and even more simply at times, through the post functionality. Pull together a few awesome paragraphs that'll get the reader hooked, and then send them through to your website with a 'read on' call to action at the end of it. Voilà, a link!

YELP

Yelp may not be as huge in this part of the world as it is elsewhere — but it's definitely worth getting your company listed there. It's quick and painless and serves as another place for people to write rave reviews about your company after you've impressed them with your product or service. It's been running in New Zealand since 2013, so there are plenty of people making use of the platform now — both potential customers and businesses. Your competition's probably on there, so you should be, too.

YELLOW

Yes, the same company who used to provide the papery brick on your doorstep each year is now a worthy presence online. It has a few different profile options, too. There are free base profiles, incorporating simple information, a logo, a description, and a ratings and review platform — and then there's the $20-a-month premium option, which also incorporates video and images, promo opportunities, social media links and more. That's some great extra oomph if your budget can swing it, but if not, the basic profile is still an important one to tick off your list.

FINDA

Finda is an excellent local directory platform, with official Google connections and better-looking profile pages than many other options. While reviewing isn't at the heart of this platform as it is on something like Yelp, it's still available as an option for users. You can list all kinds of products and/ or services that you offer, and even list the names of brands that your company has worked with or for. Just make sure that they're happy for you to do that before launching in and listing every prominent organisation you've ever done business with.

LOCALIST

Another directory whose roots were in print, like Yellow, but now functions fully online, Localist started out as an entity within New Zealand Post, but is now independent and going strong. With the tag line 'Discover local. Buy local. Love local.', there's an obvious focus on finding good stuff in your neighbourhood. So if your company fits that vibe, get signed up to Localist to integrate into its community as well as your own.

INDUSTRY DIRECTORIES

Many industries will have their own dedicated directories, whether it's something anyone can quickly register for, or something that requires official membership. If you're already the member of any organisation like that, make sure that you've got an active directory listing — and that it's up to date, with a link through to your website, of course. Also, make sure you don't get caught out with a professional directory sharing information from when you first registered, if it's no longer accurate — like if you've moved premises, changed your opening hours, or any number of other factors that can change with time.

Of course, there are many more general directory websites, and a tonne of other social media platforms, too. When it comes to directories, go wild — as long as it's a trusted source of information (a quick Google should usually highlight any scams or flash-in-the-pan organisations). Also consider leaving testimonials for other businesses or suppliers with whom you've worked, including a link back to your site in your accreditation.

For other social options, stick to platforms that you intend to actually use. If your trade is in emergency plumbing, you might not be best suited to a visual platform like Pinterest or Instagram. But on the other hand, if there are quick fixes that a layperson would be able to achieve, and you're willing to pass that information on free of charge, you could have a booming YouTube channel. But I digress — you can read up more on harnessing social media in the next chapter.

THE PULLING POWER OF GOVERNMENT AND EDUCATION

So you've ticked all the 'easy' boxes of creating your own links to your website through directories and social media accounts. Excellent. Now it's time to think about the places to channel your energy in terms of getting the most metaphorical bang for your buck as far as domain authority goes.

The top-level domain (TLD) of a website (the .com or .co. nz or .biz, etc) can play a major role in quickly identifying whether or not a website has an inherently high-ranking domain authority. And the two easiest areas to focus on are websites relating to government or higher education.

You'll see many websites highlighting the power of back links from websites with .edu and .gov TLDs. These are the TLDs for US tertiary education providers and government departments or organisations, on both a federal and state level. If your website has a relationship to the US market, and there's a feasible way to connect up with a website that's in possession of a .edu or .gov TLD, great! Perhaps you run a business that provides video-call tutoring to students anywhere in the world — there's definitely scope to connect with folks running .edu domains.

But if your market is a little closer to home, don't immediately discount the potential of government and education connections. There's still authority in .govt.nz and .ac.nz TLDs. It may be on a smaller scale than the US equivalents . . . but so too is the New Zealand market.

If you can connect in with a relevant department — whether a government one or something at a tertiary provider — you can get some of that great domain authority flowing on to your own website and up your ranking in the process. As for the how of that connection, there are plenty of ways. Maybe you can sponsor an award for a relevant faculty, or publish some really excellent content that relates well to a ministry's current cause célèbre, meaning they could link through to it in a round-up of 'useful resources'.

Get creative — it's worth the time and effort, not only for the SEO benefits, but the building of real-life, offline relationships, too! As much as we're focusing on SEO, only a fool would discount the power of word-of-mouth recommendation and support.

GETTING INTO THE PARTY

If you want to control the context of the links to your website, there's one very straightforward way to do that — share your expertise around. If you've got a connection with a company in a related field, offer to write a pro bono guest blog post. It's extra content for them, free of charge — and for you, it's the chance to share useful information on your own terms, with name recognition and a link back to your website. Everybody wins!

Want an easy option? Creating a pertinent 'how to' guide is always popular on a business blog, regardless of its focus — just make sure it relates to the intended audience. It could be how to pack for a snowboarding trip on a ski tourism website, or how to unclog a toilet on a plumbing website, or how to make sure your socks last for as long as possible on our old friend Team Sock-it's website.

You can make things even more straightforward, and offer to write a piece on the problem you had that this other company solved, why you chose them, and where to next. It's praise for the company in question while also sharing your own story.

Think about how you could create content that's related to your product, but also super-relevant for the other company you're hoping to write the post for. Maybe you're Team Sock-it and they're a design firm who created the packaging for your socks — write about why their particular design aesthetic connected with you. Maybe you're a home-building firm and they are an electrical wholesaler — write about how their products have been used to create amazing new homes for Kiwi families up and down the country. Nobody's going to complain about having someone sing their praises — just be genuine, but not simpering.

JUICING UP

'Link juice' is a phrase you might hear when you start looking into different approaches to SEO, or even just flicking through a glossary of SEO terminology online. Basically, it's the authority held by each link, that then flows (like a liquid) from one page to the next. If you have a whole lot of links coming into your page, it'll have a whole lot of link juice — but if you then link off to a whole lot of different pages from that one page, the link juice of those subsequent pages is going to be considerably less.

All that plays its role in building up the authority of your pages. Sort out your fancy inbound links to maximise the amount of link juice your pages have, and then be scrupulous with where your links lead out to. Three valuable links to other pages on your site is going to be more effective in the long run than linking every single vaguely relevant piece of information together.

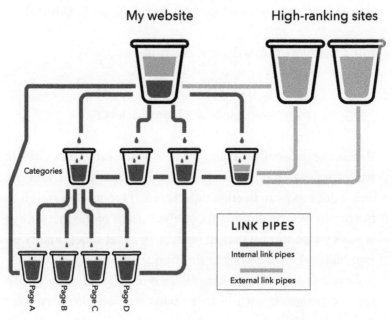

A look at link juice.

FOLLOW THE LEADER

There are some little extra elements to link tags that are important to be aware of — and one of those is the follow/nofollow element.

A follow link — which most links are by default — is an active connection between pages. The link juice flows on — whether it's diluted between other pages or not — and it does the job it's supposed to do: providing a boost to SEO.

But a nofollow link blocks up the pipes (to keep the liquid metaphor flowing).

A regular link, when rendered in HTML, looks like this:

```
<a href='https://www.teamsockit.co/'>Team Sockit</a>
```

But a nofollow link will look like this:

```
<a href='https://www.teamsockit.
co/'rel='nofollow'>Team Sockit</a>
```

While the link will still take the user to the same site, Google and other search engines are stopped in their tracks, and the link-juice food-chain ends right there. It seems a bit rough to the person you are linking to, on the surface of the matter, but it plays an important part in healthy internet functionality — especially when it comes to limiting spam.

At one point in time, many blogs would be inundated with spam comments, with links to whatever website they were trying to spruik. If you were linking to valuable content in the body of your blog, that link was competing for link juice with whatever else cropped up in the comments. But the introduction of the nofollow tag meant a major drop-off in spam comments, after websites like WordPress defaulted to sticking the nofollow tag on all links in comments. You can do this on your site if you've got the right setting in your CMS, otherwise ask your web developer to do it (if it's not in place already). It's worth it, as less visual spam = great. Less diluted link juice = even better.

KEEPING THE HOUSE CLEAN

Make sure to regularly check in on inbound links that you're aware of, and the websites that they are coming from. Some companies ultimately don't go the distance — or may outright change what they do. If a company you once wrote a blog for is now going down a path that you're not necessarily comfortable with, you might want to look at asking them to take the post down. You agreed to provide them with content in good faith that they were a certain type of business — and now they aren't.

It's also a good reminder to check the links on your own site, to make sure that they are connecting to sites that are still active, rather than 404 error pages, or redirecting to generic homepages.

If you have the patience for it, this technique can be extended beyond your own site, to your advantage. Think of it this way. You're Team Sock-it, and you're having a look on the internet for the company that provides your raw materials, Great Yarnz. They have a blog post about different ways their product is used, with links to examples. But the link in the apparel paragraph leads to a 404 page on a competitor's website.

Why not send a friendly message to Great Yarnz, like the following?

Dear Stuart,

I've just been reading your blog – loving that the content you put out is so consistently useful to a company like ours! But I did notice that on your post Great Yarnz On

The Go, the link in the apparel section isn't working. I'd love to write up an informal case study about how we use your product on our own blog, which you could link through to without actually changing anything on your post except for the link itself. How does that sound?

Looking forward to our next catch-up,
Jessie

When it comes to inbound linking, the web really is a self-perpetuating popularity contest. The more other websites you can convince of your worthiness to link to, the more links you'll generate. And the more valuable links pointing to you, the more Google will push you up the rankings. It's a no-brainer — capture those links, and you'll continue to work your way towards that top spot on the search-results page. Stay in people's good books online and offline, and it'll pay off in every way!

CASE STUDY: THE IMPORTANCE OF LINKS TO PURE SEO'S OWN SEO STRATEGY

Pure SEO's own link-building journey is a good example of the power of links as part of an SEO strategy. As a new business, with a new website in a country where I had no previous work experience or network, Pure SEO had not yet established any authority or credibility in the market. In the early days, my focus on link building was similar to my approach to building the business generally, which I shared at the start of the book: I just needed to get out there.

Right from the outset, my goal was to get to number one on Google for the term 'Search Engine Optimisation' in New Zealand. To me, this is what proves that we know what we're doing; we have to be walking the talk. It took us 18 months to get there – again proving that real results don't happen overnight – but we reached that top spot in 2011 and have remained in the top three ever since.

A look at our 'Search Console' results shows the number of times each term was searched for on Google in the last month (impressions) and the amount of times our site was clicked on, as well as our average ranking position over this period.

	Queries	Clicks ▼	Impressions	Position	
1	pure seo ⌐	441	1,058	1.0	⟩
2	pureseo ⌐	251	473	1.0	⟩
3	seo ⌐	79	5,154	5.6	⟩
4	seo nz ⌐	53	710	1.1	⟩
5	seo auckland ⌐	42	1,039	2.7	⟩
6	google adwords ⌐	29	15,464	7.5	⟩
7	richard conway ⌐	25	54	1.1	⟩
8	pure seo wellington ⌐	23	38	1.0	⟩
9	pure seo nz ⌐	17	29	1.0	⟩

So, how did our link-building strategy help us take the top spots?

Low-hanging fruit

The beginning for us was all about the low-hanging fruit, and I would certainly recommend this as a place to start. This is all the stuff that you can achieve easily while you are first building your brand: including your business on directories and local listings, with a link back to your site.

Think about the relationships you have in the real world and consider whether a link from a supplier or distributor is appropriate. Memberships in networking groups or industry organisations also tend to create a link back to your site. Could you enter a relevant business award, take on a speaking event or sponsor something related to your field (or just in an area of interest)? All of these things generate legitimate links.

RICHARD CONWAY

SEO Auckland - Pure SEO
09 950 3888
Email >
Follow us on
(f) (y) (in) (g+)

VISIT WEBSITE

Richard Conway (centre) From Pure SEO On The
Google Engage Experts Panel

This was a great link as a result of a speaking opportunity. Not only does this have an effect on Google as it crawls the web legitimising us, but it lends us credibility for humans that happen upon it, too. As do things like our inclusion in the Deloitte Fast 500 Business Awards for the Asia-Pacific region:

Outreach

Next came active outreach. Here we thought about sites that we could contribute content to. We looked to others in our industry, or closely related ones, and offered to write content for other people's blogs, industry publications and sites. Inevitably, these are then linked back to us in their accreditation.

"We are a very culture led organisation; the key to our successful growth is in our hiring policy. We hire predominantly on attitude; people can learn new skills, but it is very hard to teach attitude. I was lucky enough to spend a week recently with Richard Branson on his private island (Necker Island), he also shared this view. We have a very low attrition rate at Pure SEO and we believe that is down to the great team we have here." **Richard Conway, CEO, Pure SEO The Search Engine**

Richard Conway - **Founder at Pure SEO**

SEO during 2017 is going to see a further shift towards user focussed factors. Many SEO people expose the overused soundbite "content is king", however, in our view this is not correct; the "customer is king". If you think about it, the only reason people keep coming back to Google is they are served results that are relevant to them.

If all aspects of your content, UI and marketing have a core customer focus you are unlikely to go wrong in

One thing we did, which I would highly recommend, was create a database of sites to which you can contribute thoughts. Being active (in a value-based and not spammy way) on forums can also result in relevant links.

On that note, it doesn't always have to be one person from the organisation, be it the CEO or another figurehead, that's creating content – get different members of your team involved, as every link counts.

Here's an example from Brett Langlois from our team:

zacjohnson.com   **57 Entrepreneurs Share their Favorite Entrepreneur Success Quotes**

My favorite quote about success is an old one attributed to Thomas
Edison. Although the exact wording is in dispute, the story goes that
when asked by a reporter about the incredible difficulties he faced when
finding a suitable filament for the light bulb, Edison responded, *"I have
not failed once. I've just found 10,000 ways that don't work."*

This quote reveals the importance of learning from "failures" and
reframing them as successes. Failure is an inevitable part of life, and the
most important thing is to grow from it. If you can reframe "I failed at this" to "I succeeded in
learning not to do this", it will keep you motivated on your way to where you want to go and
discourage you from giving up.

Brett Langlois – Pure SEO

We also invest in promoting great pieces of content
that we create, which often results in organic links
– people writing their own pieces about the topic
and referring to (and linking to) something we have
already said. You can see how this strategy really starts
getting legs of its own.

Content

Somewhat related to the idea of outreach, but taking
a slightly different form, is other content. For us, this
is about regularly contributing content for use by the
media, and actively doing PR related to the company.
In New Zealand, I regularly write for *NZ Business* and
M2 magazines, as well as appearing in regular articles
in *The New Zealand Herald*, on Stuff.co.nz and the like.
Back in 2014, I had the opportunity through
Entrepreneurs Organization, as part of an invited

group of entrepreneurs, to go to Necker Island to hang out with Richard Branson for the week. While this was a fantastic opportunity to meet – and spend time with – someone I admired, I have to admit that the main attraction for me was that I knew it would generate us some great PR.

Major news pages get high volumes of traffic, so links from these sorts of sites are hugely valuable, both for general exposure, and to Google.

BUSINESS

Richard Conway: What I learned in the company of Richard Branson

8 Aug, 2014 9:30am

⏱ 5 minutes to reac

Richard Conway spent a few days on Sir Richard Branson's Caribbean island with a group of tech entrepreneurs.

We have to keep doing it, but it gets easier

From our proactive and self-led link strategy, our activity to maintain our position has changed over the years. In the maintenance phase, so many more of our links happen organically. Having established ourselves as thought leaders in the search space, we're approached now for comments and content, which we happily contribute, simply asking that they link back to us when they credit our thoughts.

Although the value that Google places on different links has changed over the years we have been doing this, the overall strategy remains valid: links still work like a vote for your web page, and these votes help with ranking.

What not to do

Thankfully, because our focus from the outset has been on ethical SEO – doing the work to get the genuine, hard-won results – we stayed well away from the dodgy things that lots of others were doing to get links. Buying links, making pages just for links . . . these approaches are bad news. One supplier I knew back in those early days was creating an extra page on each of his clients' websites and using these to link all the sites to each other. However, Google is quick to detect patterns and ultimately penalises those trying to cheat the system. Even reciprocal linking, the idea of 'you link to me in exchange for me linking to you', is frowned upon nowadays.

CHAPTER SUMMARY

» Links are a critical part of SEO – arguably
  even more important than keywords!

» Sort out directory listings and appropriate
  social media profiles for inbound links that
  you have maximum control over.

» Understand that some websites are stronger than
  others when it comes to domain authority. Google
  loves education and government websites.

» Create content for other companies and websites
  to create inbound links on your own terms.

» Soak up all the link juice you can – but don't dilute it by
  going wild with too many links on your own pages.

THIRTEEN:

SO WHAT ABOUT SOCIAL?

It would be crazy — and probably impossible — to try to create a guide to anything in the digital marketing space in this day and age without touching on social media and the role that it plays. As Larry Kim, CEO of Facebook Messenger marketing platform MobileMonkey and founder of search-marketing company WordStream says, 'Our experiments show that search and social marketing are changing more than ever.'

SEO definitely has a relationship with social media that's worth highlighting — a relationship that has both direct and indirect elements. But the first thing to know is that this isn't a case of the simplest answer being the correct one. Despite the fact that it might seem as though a larger social following should equal a higher ranking on Google, it's just not the case, or at least, it's certainly not as straightforward as that.

As Larry Kim adds, 'There are a lot of theories about how social media affects SEO. However, my tests have found that the more social engagement, the more clicks from organic search. Instead of spreading yourself thin in areas with little return — I call these donkeys — find unicorn opportunities that result in 95 per cent of the reward.'

So let's look into what is going on and where the unicorns may be hiding.

WHAT PLATFORMS SHOULD I BE ON?

Social media is a minefield for the unwary. It can feel very hard to know what platforms are worth your time and which ones aren't — and everything gets thrown for a loop when another new platform suddenly appears. I touched on some details about different social avenues in the last chapter — particularly Facebook and LinkedIn. But it's time to look more closely, and to look at ongoing usage, rather than just that initial set-up.

Remember, this isn't a recommendation that you go out and start trying to tackle and conquer every single platform that's available. Instead, think about what you want to get from your social presence, and the time and energy you have to expend towards this part of your business's marketing.

FACEBOOK

A reported 2.9 million New Zealanders, 15 million Australians and 2 billion people worldwide can't be wrong. Facebook offers flexibility in what kinds of content you can present to your followers, from video to text to photos to in-situ, visually interesting articles. There's powerful advertising and business functionality available to users too, so if you're looking at spending money to generate leads or just likes for your page, there's plenty of tinkering that you can do to get in front of the appropriate people.

TWITTER

Twitter is more popular among some groups of the population than others — so do a bit of research to see whether you're likely to strike a chord or not. In New Zealand, the dominant themes are political discourse and people engaged in creative and cultural communities — as well as, of course, a sizeable number of tech folks. And don't forget the up-at-1 a.m.-for-feeding parent Twitter community!

You'll need to master the art of being concise and engaging, and speedy in responding to tweets. While the previous character limit of 140 has doubled to 280 in recent times, it's still the platform for rapid-fire conversations and sharing of opinions — and you have to make sure you can be heard above all of the noise.

INSTAGRAM

For photos and short snappy video, Instagram is definitely a platform to be on — as long as those photos and snappy videos are beautiful or otherwise visually interesting. It doesn't have to be exquisite images of all your products laid out, or of luscious sunsets — but it should be well-composed images taken with a decent camera (decent phone cameras do, of course, count!). It's also owned by Facebook, which makes interconnectivity between the two apps nice and painless. You can create posts on Instagram that seamlessly get shared on Facebook — and you can easily include Instagram as an option when developing advertising with Facebook's tool.

LINKEDIN

LinkedIn is an obvious choice for anyone who runs a B2B-focused company. You're getting connected to people while they're in work mode — and you can see what kinds of positions they are in, so you know whether you're resonating with people in the right roles and in the right industries.

You're probably safe to stick to the platform best suited to your business of these four. There's an argument to be made for Pinterest too, but that's suited to a very niche range of industries, and it doesn't have quite the same numbers locally. Google+ involvement can mostly tie into your Google My Business page and posts, which we've covered already. YouTube is considered by some to be a social media platform but, for business purposes, it really functions as a video hosting and discovery platform, rather than a place to engage in a conversation with your customers, whether current or potential.

And beyond — there's more than you could really imagine. Tumblr, Flickr, WhatsApp, Snapchat . . . and that's before you take into account the millions of users on Chinese platforms like WeChat and Weibo. But for the purposes of this book and this chapter in particular, when I'm talking about social platforms, I'm talking about Facebook, Instagram, LinkedIn and Twitter.

THE SYMBIOSIS OF SOCIAL AND SEARCH

For Linda Coles of Blue Banana, SEO is an integral part of her arsenal. As a marketing professional focused on social media and content creation, she understands the importance of working in a space where social and SEO are aligned. She also writes thrillers – so she knows a thing or two about marketing both her own products and those of clients in different ways!

'Websites have been around forever, and social has been around for what seems like forever, but is actually only really a good ten years. Websites are tried and true – and all social drives back to a website,' Coles says. 'In those early days of social media, everyone was all about gathering connections, no matter how tenuous – a race for us all to see who could max out at five thousand first. But times change – and so have our social habits.'

Coles notes that Google is constantly working in the background, changing its algorithms and its focus from week to week. 'And the question is whether or not they take into account what is happening on social. But social drives traffic back,' she says – which inherently affects how things rank in search.

'That widget you want to sell, the service you're trying to sell – in order to do any of that these days, either you have to spend money on advertising or write content and share it via social. But the question is then, what do you write about that will attract people – on Facebook, on LinkedIn, and maybe on Instagram and the other platforms?'

THE OFFICIAL WORD FROM GOOGLE

Since 2014, Google has claimed that social media has no impact on its ranking algorithm. Matt Cutts, then the tech giant's head of web spam, put out a video explaining its reasoning. Basically, it considered that the changeable nature of social media meant it was an unreliable source of signals. As such, it couldn't be depended on for ongoing and accurate information.

Despite Google's official position, there are many different ways that people and businesses have found that social media does, in fact, play its part in affecting search ranking — just not necessarily in an immediately obvious way. The team at Hootsuite, a widely used social media scheduling tool, ran an experiment in early 2018, where a group of inbound marketing, data analytics and social marketing teams joined forces and took to Twitter. They organised a set of pre-existing blog posts into three different groups — a control group, with no social media sharing; an organic group, with links to the articles shared on Twitter; and a paid promo group, with links to the articles shared on Twitter with a paid boost.

The ultimate result was that the control group saw no change in search visibility, the organic group saw 12 per cent growth and the paid promo group saw 22 per cent growth in their search visibility. That's nothing to be sniffed at — and definitely suggests that social media is playing some sort of a role.

It's also worth mentioning, of course, that what is the case now won't necessarily be the case forever. So even if we ignore the results of experiments like this one, and take Google at its word, you can never be sure what shifts in approach and algorithms may come with time. Better to take a careful and considered approach to how SEO and social could and might intersect now, and be in a powerful position if Google changes tack, rather than wave it off as unimportant and be left in the lurch should such a change take place.

Ultimately, it's good digital housekeeping to be thoughtful and consistent across your web presence — you might as well take a little time and do things properly, whatever the end result may be. And let's not forget to highlight search engine Bing in this instance, which has confirmed that it does officially take social media into account in the development of its rankings. It's not a huge factor, but it does play its part.

THE LINK LINK

One school of thought when it comes to seeing the impact that social media seems to have on search results is the fact that creating a post with a link to an article is invoking one of the core tenets of this whole SEO enterprise — links. So regardless of what claimed connection, or lack thereof, there is between social media platforms and Google rankings, posts on social are driving inbound links, and people are clicking them.

There's also a potential extra useful link avenue for users browsing social platforms on their phones. Each of the main four platforms has an in-app browser — so if you click a link in a tweet or in someone's Instagram bio or story, instead of being transported out to Safari or Chrome or whatever other internet app your phone runs, you'll be using a bespoke browser within the app itself.

Usually, these browser functionalities will also make things as easy as possible for further sharing. So if someone clicks on a blog post you've shared in a tweet and then has a look through your other articles, if they come across one that really resonates with them, it's a quick and easy couple of taps for them to then share that article with their own network. This gives you a whole extra link, to up that inbound volume.

Of course, social is about more than just words — and Linda Coles of Blue Banana is a proponent of ways to use visual and multimedia elements without reinventing the wheel.

'You can use the same information but in a visual way for other platforms. Evergreen content can be developed in different ways. Record an audio, put it on LinkedIn. Make a video, put it on YouTube. Make images, put them on Instagram. Put it all into a downloadable document.' The crux is to tailor to the platform, rather than take the 'spray and pray' approach.

'And it's got to be interesting, even though not all products are sexy or glamorous,' Coles says. She presents the example of one of her clients, a glass company — not necessarily the sort of organisation that you'd expect to be killing it on social media. But it made a 15-minute video on the future of glass, which got really good engagement. Now, some 10 years after the video was originally created, some of the things that the company predicted have become part of our lives — demonstrating to potential customers today that they know their stuff, both today and tomorrow.

Another example among Linda Coles's clients is Life Care Consultants, based in Hamilton.

'I'd been working on their social media for quite some time, but for a long time they didn't have a very good website —

then it finally materialised.' The change was significant —
not only was it modern and relevant, but it included news
and blog areas so that all kinds of areas of expertise could be
highlighted in different ways, from wellness to general health
and safety.

'There was lots of useful content on there that was easy to
link to,' Coles adds, highlighting again the vital importance
of that linkable content. 'And it was created in a way that
meant you didn't feel like you were being sold to — instead,
it talked about issues like mental health in the workplace.'
Here we see again that it's all about thoughtful, purposeful
and linkable content.

'They don't see their website as a dusty brochure in the sky
— it's now something that generates money for them,' Coles
says. It's that idea of your website functioning as your welcome
desk and the receptionist behind it all in one — it needs to be
slick and informative.

Social is an area of constant change — just like Google's
algorithms. Coles specifically notes the change a couple of
years back on Facebook, when reliance on organic traffic was
no longer tenable for the vast majority of businesses. Organic
content is necessary, and can yield good results — but for
real cut-through on social these days, it is pay to play. Coles
is quick to mention, however, that it doesn't have to mean
spending a lot — just spending carefully.

QUALITY CONTROL

At this point, you're hopefully on board with the idea that
Google is really a fan of quality, rather than just messes of
keywords crushed together. And this is another place that

social can come to the SEO party. Content that is shared via social media at just the right moment — managing to capture likes and shares and engaged commenters — is a great mark of quality.

Not only that, but if you really hit the nail on the head, you might end up reaching other creators and influencers who will in turn share your content, further pushing those links back to your website. More than that, though, powerful influencers will carry greater rank authority — as discussed in chapter 12 — so will boost your ranking potential in more ways than just sheer numbers.

Linda Coles is a big supporter of a pillar-based approach to web content, which serves both the search and social sides of marketing equally well. Hailing back to around 2006, the train of thought is that if you create four pillars of content, you'll have the structure to hold the 'building' up — the building in this case being the integrity of your website. The pillars guide the creation of the rest of your content, both on your website and across your social media platforms. They are the four main things that you need to communicate or get across, which will be different for everyone. For example, if you are a construction company you might want to cover your construction expertise, the machinery or methods you primarily use, after-sales support, and a case study story that sees you shine.

'The first thing you want to do is think about that pillar content and what you want it to be — and then break it down from there. There will be lots of little subjects that come underneath each pillar,' Coles explains.

'Putting content on your website and sharing it is the goal, and the best place to start is with your frequently asked questions. What do your customers continuously ask you? That's going to be a pillar of content. Do you distribute nationwide? If so, write a blog about it, and share that blog on your social platforms.'

In her own recent development of her presence online as an author, Coles used those FAQs as a starting point. The pillars for a crime fiction author might be the books themselves, the recurring characters in the series, where the books are available, and information about the author.

From there, the subjects develop. Once you look into the characters, you might wonder whether or not you need to read from the beginning of the series in order to understand character development and plot movement. So that becomes another piece of content, on both your website and your social accounts — do I need to read the books in order? Is it a trilogy? Are all the books in the series already released? Each of those points can create a post, anywhere from four or five hundred words upwards. You'll have a sense of what the attention span of your target customers is like.

HANDLING YOUR HORSES

Let's say you've got a company that lends itself to an ongoing visual story as well as a text-based one, and you've also noticed that a lot of your competitors seem to be active on Twitter. That's Facebook, Instagram and Twitter without breaking a sweat. So how, then, do you handle running three different social media accounts while also doing everything else on your plate?

For many people, the answer will lie in using a scheduling tool of some kind. Hootsuite has already been mentioned, but other tools like Buffer and Sprout are also popular. Basically, you connect all your social accounts to this one platform, which enables you to use one single dashboard to schedule your posts and undertake varying levels of monitoring and management.

If there's one post that you know you want to blast across all your platforms, a tool like this can be a lifesaver. Rather than logging into each profile separately — including getting your phone out to post to Instagram — you can do it all in one place, with one core post that you can tailor to each platform as necessary.

Remember that the posts themselves are indexable and searchable by Google — so this is another time to think about what you've learnt as far as what works and doesn't on the keyword front. Instead of 'An update on our visit to Sydney for XYZ Conference', why not make the text of your post 'Our 9 top lessons from the 2018 XYZ Conference — and our 3 recommendations of what to do with a spare afternoon in Sydney!'.

Linda Coles offers the following story about a car dealership. Volkswagen opened a small concept store in Pukekohe, south of Auckland — very small. You'd think they wouldn't be able to sell many cars with so little space, but that turned out to not be a problem.

Firstly, the facility itself had technology that allowed potential buyers to see the interior and exterior of every VW car, but beyond that useful element, it seems buyers aren't so dependent on the physical any more. The average person used to visit a car yard 6 times prior to making a purchase, but now it's only 1.5 times. People research online — the only thing they need from the physical encounter is to see the colour in real life and take a test drive.

If anything similar to that figure change — 6 to 1.5 — can be seen in other industries, it really highlights just how important online visibility and calibre of web presence are to ensure that people can find you and trust you as a critical part of the research process. It's where people are, and where we're looking, so social plays an important role within that.

CHAPTER SUMMARY

» Social media is an integral part of the digital marketing equation, regardless of what your main focus is.

» Different platforms lend themselves to different kinds of businesses. Take that into consideration before signing up for everything you come across.

» Even if Google doesn't officially acknowledge social media as a contributing factor to its algorithm, the links driven by social still play a part.

» Use appropriate keywords where possible to maximise the indexable nature of social media platforms.

» Make use of scheduling tools if you have multiple platforms to manage.

FOURTEEN:

SUPERCHARGE YOUR SEO

As you'll already be starting to see, there is a lot that you can do beyond your own website to improve your search-ranking results. The technical foundation of on-page SEO is important, but it's in off-page SEO that non-techies can come into their own.

Remember how I said that successful SEO is really just good marketing? Well, here is where I'll prove that yet again. Get your marketing mind engaged, because now is when you'll have the opportunity to supercharge your SEO.

You've seen the way that SEO integrates with your other marketing, the importance of legitimate links that act as a vote for your website or web page, and the impact of social media. In this chapter we'll consider how other activities such as PR and the use of influencers can help with search marketing. Let's start by unpacking those terms.

PUTTING THE SPOTLIGHT ON PUBLIC RELATIONS

At its most basic level, PR is what its acronym suggests: public relations. It's the process by which you relate to your public, your targets and your audience. More specifically, it's the way you manage the spread of information about your brand or business to the public.

In essence, PR puts your brand or business in the spotlight for the positive purpose of enabling you to manage its reputation. It's about gaining understanding and support, as well as trying to influence opinions and behaviour. And it takes a range of forms.

Traditionally, public relations was all about utilising the traditional media to communicate — directly or indirectly — with your target audience. It's an effective method of communication if you have a compelling narrative that goes beyond just a features list of your product or service. It's the opportunity to highlight your brand story, share your values or convey a particular lifestyle.

It also differs from advertising in that it occupies the realm of editorial, which was historically thought to carry greater influence or credibility for the fact that the mention wasn't paid for. More recently the lines on this have blurred, however.

The reach of what is considered the realm of PR has also changed. The point of PR is to connect with your intended audience, so you need to do that through the channels that have their eyes and ears. As the traditional news media has lost audience to other channels, these other channels — such as social media, forums or podcasts — have become a more and more valid space for PR activity. It's this, too, that has given rise to the age of influencer marketing.

WHAT IS INFLUENCER MARKETING?

Influencer marketing is defined as a form of marketing where the focus is placed on influential people, as opposed to the target market as a whole. It's about using these so-called 'influencers' as the vehicle by which to be seen by your target audience. From a PR perspective, you're trying to win over the influencer to rave positively about your product or service as, once they are doing so, they will hopefully win over the followers who make up their audience — such is their influence.

Whether they've established themselves as an authority in a particular area (and hence have the: 'well, she would know — she's an expert' credibility), or made themselves relatable to a particular group (with 'she's another mum like me' influence), influencer marketing creates the ultimate 'ripple effect'. The majority of this activity is happening in the social space; some influencers can move the market at the speed of a tweet!

Influencer marketing tends to occupy that place between official testimonials and passing product mentions. It's hyper-targeted exposure which is, at its core, about leveraging a key person's audience for your brand. The influencer does some of the hard work for you, as consumers are interested in, and paying attention to, the influencers that they've chosen to follow. Not only that, they're more likely to trust their recommendations than those put out by a business or brand itself. And, if done well, the positive influence snowballs.

Once potentially the domain of PR, the use of influencers has more recently moved into the marketing sphere —

differentiated by the exchange of money for mentions, or what are otherwise known as 'sponsored posts'. Paid or otherwise, though, influencer marketing looks to be here to stay. According to a study by influencer marketing platform Linqia of close to 200 marketers, across a range of sectors in the United States, 86 per cent used influencer marketing in 2017 and 92 per cent of those found it to be effective.

Closer to home, all indications point to the fact that it's similarly alive and well in New Zealand. As entrepreneur Iyia Liu, one of the biggest success stories of influencer marketing from our shores, says, 'Influencer marketing is a very powerful tool. The world is more connected now than ever over social media, so why not use it as a platform to reach people?

'More and more people are catching on to the increase in influencer marketing, with a lot of traditional marketing forms transitioning — for example, PR companies who once focused on traditional media now opt to send product to influencers and throw influencer events, or traditional news outlets that once published in newspapers and magazines now focus their content on Facebook.'

However, this isn't just a lesson in influencer marketing — it's a look at how this method can be used specifically to amplify your search-marketing results. So how do these avenues impact search? And how can you leverage them as part of your SEO strategy?

PR AND INFLUENCER MARKETING'S IMPACT ON SEARCH

Remember how I said back in chapter 12 that you want to establish a variety of credible links to your site to help when

Google sets its rankings? The quality and authority of sites that link to you are among the top search-ranking factors, after all. However, some claim that it's getting increasingly difficult to generate links. It's here that PR and the use of influencers can have a significant impact, enabling you to earn links from other high-authority domains that are relevant to your site.

Working with influencers, or having your business or brand featured in the news media (hopefully in a positive way, but this isn't actually essential in this instance!), is a great way to generate natural back links for your site, to further improve your site ranking. There are a few ways that this happens. In some cases, you might work with influencers who have their own website, with a blog for example. If not, it's likely they'll have access to some other digital channel, like their Facebook feed or Instagram account, that has high authority with Google because of the sort of traffic they are getting. The key thing is high engagement — as Google values this greatly. When these influencers create content on social media, blogs and vlogs and link it back to you, they're not only getting the word out, they're creating a quality link.

Think of link building as an online popularity contest — each link is a vote, effectively. Because of their authority, an influencer sharing your link increases the chances of other people sharing that link (more votes), so your reach, and link collecting, can extend that way.

According to a Moz study, the quantity and quality of social shares are among the top nine ranking factors for your website, too. The more popularity your link has, the greater the chances too of other even higher-authority domains — like the news media — picking it up; this is the allure of something going viral.

Not only does it get seen by more eyeballs, it gets viewed more favourably by Google.

UPPING YOUR CONTENT GAME

We've covered the necessity of high-quality content for SEO already, and I also made the point that you don't have to generate all of your content yourself. Influencer marketing helps with this. Influencers are individuals whose key role is to create captivating, shareable content on a brand or business's behalf, which is a huge help in and of itself in the challenge to always come up with fresh content ideas.

Influencers can also leverage their followers to produce content for you, whether by encouraging their community to share their own thoughts or images, or amplifying engagement with one of your campaign hashtags. Either way, user-generated content has huge value and further raises awareness and ranking — helping to do some of the heavy lifting of content generation.

BEING SEEN AND HEARD ABOVE THE NOISE

One of the biggest challenges, in all realms of digital marketing, is how to be seen and heard amid your sea of competitors. Engagement and site traffic is the fifth most important ranking factor (also according to the aforementioned Moz study), so a great SEO result depends on engaging your audience and achieving higher traffic.

Obviously, exposure is going to up your game in this regard. Influencers will have a massive following and significant reach of their own, which naturally improves the visibility of your content and business — and increases the chances of attracting potential visitors to your website. However, it's the 'influence' part of influencer marketing that really amplifies the results. The specific group that an influencer is talking to are actively following and engaging with them; they're hanging off their every product review and recommendation.

In further good news, people trust people ahead of ads. Recent research by advertising agency Ogilvy and Google found that 74 per cent of consumers identify word of mouth as a key factor in their purchasing decisions. In most cases, people trust influencers almost as much as they trust their friends, which is why they're so effective at getting you results.

So, we can see that it's worthwhile to leverage relevant influencers' communities to enhance your business or brand's visibility and engagement. Let's get started . . .

TIPS AND TRICKS FOR UTILISING PR AND INFLUENCERS FOR SEARCH

Finding relevant, authoritative influencers is the most important aspect of influencer marketing. So how do you know who you're looking for?

FIND A TARGET TO UNLOCK YOUR TARGET

Think about your intended audience or target market: what are the people you are targeting reading, watching or doing online? What bloggers do they follow? Where are they putting their attention? What do they do in their spare time? What other interests might they have in common?

Then consider whether there is anyone who is considered an authority or 'rock star' in that space.

You can find some of this out by simply asking your customers and prospects — send out a survey. Or, if you'd like to let your fingers do the walking, so to speak, conduct your own research. Run a Twitter search or a hashtag search on a related topic and see which voices show up plentifully, and who seems to be inspiring a reaction and engendering trust. The trick here is that you're trying to find influencers who hold sway with your intended target market.

When you identify an influencer who you think would be good for your business or brand, drill down to their audience demographics. What's the age, gender and location of those who are following them? Does that align with your target?

LOOK PAST SOME OF THE NUMBERS

Don't simply get seduced by how many followers an influencer has; this is another area where quality trumps sheer quantity. Sometimes the smaller influencers with a more niche following can even be more beneficial.

The rules of good marketing apply here and if you've got limited budget to achieve great results, you don't want to be taking a generic approach with the widest possible audience. Their reach or follower numbers isn't the be-all and end-all; what you also want to consider is how much engagement they have.

MAKE SURE THEY'VE GOT ENGAGEMENT

The traffic that influencers drive to your site can boost your

SEO rankings in ways that paid ads sometimes cannot. But their content has to be getting engagement for this to happen. Check what sort of engagement an influencer gets per post. Posts from people with small followings can get really strong engagement, bringing authenticity and building trust among both humans and Google bots. As I mentioned, an influencer with two million followers may not always be as powerful as a micro-influencer in your niche who has, say, only 30,000 (highly engaged) followers.

CREATE A PLAN OF ATTACK

Once you've identified some influencers, build a spreadsheet list that you are able to update and prioritise. When it comes to ranking them, consider those things we've just explored above — who is their audience: is it your primary or secondary target? How many followers do they have? What sort of engagement does their content get? Once you compare these variables, you'll be able to see where you could focus your energy and budget.

REACH OUT AND RESEARCH

Take your list of top influencers and subscribe to or follow them yourself. Spend some time engaging with, liking and sharing the material that they share that resonates with you. But be genuine about it. You're looking to form a relationship, and those go two ways.

When it comes to engaging, don't go into a conversation in full sales mode. Share what you are doing in a way that invites them to offer their opinions, participate for themselves, or suggest people from their community to put forward for testing a new product, for example. You're looking for the win-win here; they need to feel as though they're getting something too, so take the time to understand what they're about.

Influencers have taken time and energy to build their audience and establish trust with them, so most are selective about the brands and businesses they work with. It's up to you to understand these people and determine how you can deliver their audience something of value, as that's their core purpose. Treat these people as partners, and show you value and respect their role, and you'll get much greater results.

LOOK FOR ORGANIC OPPORTUNITIES

In many cases, where you engage in paid influencer marketing, the influencers will disclose that a mention (and its accompanying link) are sponsored. You don't have to have an influencer create what is effectively their own commercial (be it video or visual) for your brand or business directly. Get creative and consider, or talk to them about, the option of a campaign related to a specific issue in your industry. Instead of this containing direct sales messages, it might be more about their thoughts on a topic, citing your site as a resource. This may be a way to bypass the need for it to be labelled as a paid post.

On that note, work together with the influencers who you target, and trust that they have a much deeper understanding of their communities and what works or is well received by their fans and followers. You'll have your own objectives in mind, but take their input on board in terms of what will be effective. Of course you're looking to leverage the power of word of mouth, but ultimately you're both looking to build organic, authentic and trustworthy conversations.

GO THE DISTANCE

My last piece of advice here is to accept that leveraging influencer marketing and PR is like good SEO itself: a long-term play. It's not a quick fix, nor is it as simple as just connecting up with a few people in various corners of the internet and then waiting for the results to roll in. They're also not silver bullets, but they can be powerful tools in your SEO arsenal if you develop a clear strategy and integrate it with your social media and content-marketing strategies and other search activities.

Get clear on what you want to achieve, set measurable objectives and constantly measure the performance and impact of your activity, so you can continuously tweak and improve.

CASE STUDY: WAIST TRAINER NZ AUS, AN INFLUENCER SUCCESS STORY

As I said earlier in this chapter, Iyia Liu is one of the biggest success stories in influencer marketing from our shores – going from one Facebook page and next to no marketing budget to a company turning over more than $3.5 million in the last financial year. If there were any doubts about the power of influencers, Liu allayed them.

At just 23 years of age, recent commerce graduate and savvy social media fanatic Liu discovered a corset-style belt designed to help women emulate the coveted hourglass figure. 'I personally wanted the product,' Liu admits. 'I tried it and liked it, so thought if I liked it, maybe other girls like me would like it too.'

From there, she put her entrepreneurial ambition and $6000 of savings to work; Waist Trainer NZ Aus was born. She got a first batch made and delivered from China and started on marketing them – using Facebook and Instagram, of course.

'I found the Waist Trainer product through an influencer, so I thought if I found it this way, why shouldn't I try to sell them this way?' As her own intended target audience, this was sound logic, and it worked. The orders started rolling in, and soon she had eight staff members and a business that far exceeded the online boutique she originally started as a side project.

The real kicker came when Liu invested a six-figure sum in a celebrity (influencer) endorsement. The Instagram photograph of Kylie Jenner wearing the waist trainer received 1.5 million likes and almost 300,000 comments. Sales leads were tracked through the promo code 'Kylie' that purchasers entered when they ordered. Although the influencer investment paid off, Liu admits 'the return was not as fast as I thought it would be'.

'I think influencer marketing is so effective because people can relate to it,' she adds. ' Sometimes I'll see a product on a website but won't be totally convinced that I need or want it. Then I'll often see it on an influencer and be adamant I need it. It helps to build consumer trust.'

When it comes to choosing an influencer, Liu believes the most important factor is relevancy to your brand.

'Think about whether their followers would be able to relate or would be interested. There's no point having an influencer with millions of followers promote a female-oriented product if their following is predominantly male, or vice versa. Likewise, there's no point having an influencer who has an international audience if your product is restricted to a certain location.' This reinforces the idea that having huge numbers of followers for the sake of followers isn't everything.

Liu cautions to beware of paying influencers who don't do the work.

'Have a clear brief of what you want posted and analyse whether their account is authentic and their engagement is real. I know of people who have paid "influencers" with thousands of followers who have effectively just bought fake followers.' Make sure you're not paying for inflated numbers that aren't going to deliver the results.

CHAPTER SUMMARY

» Public relations and influencer marketing enable
  you to amplify your SEO efforts for better results.

» PR and influencer marketing can be a source
  of additional, high-quality links.

» Do your research. Like good marketing,
  utilising influencers relies on drilling down to,
  and understanding, your target market.

» Look past just the numbers of followers for real, genuine
  engagement, as that's what will really bring the results.

FIFTEEN:
METRICS AND MEASUREMENT

It's one thing to follow guidance, play by the rules and put into place an incredible SEO campaign. It's another to figure out whether or not it's working the way you're hoping it will.

As with all things in business, it's necessary to figure out some methods of measurement and analysis to keep track of changes and developments — and, hopefully, progress. There's nothing wrong with feeling pleased that you've implemented all the changes you planned, and having a sense that things are improving — but solid figures to back that up are going to do more convincing than positive feelings could ever really hope to.

Right off the bat, it's good to remember that there are a whole lot of ideas and perspectives out there on what the best metrics to track are, and how best to go about doing that. No two businesses have identical goals and objectives and, as such, no two businesses will have precisely the same reporting needs from their SEO measurement and metrics. If I suggest something here that doesn't feel relevant to your business, don't stress. There's no cookie-cutter method that can be perfectly replicated for each different organisation — just use your intuition and a bit of professional guidance along the way!

WHERE THE MAGIC HAPPENS: GOOGLE ANALYTICS 101

The good news is that one place that is dependably full of just the kind of information you'll want when creating reports and assessing trends lies with our good friend Google. Google Analytics is a powerful tool and the first port of call for most people when it comes to understanding search traffic to their websites.

KICKING THINGS OFF

Got a Google account? Great. Not sure? If you've ever created a Gmail account, or even a YouTube account, you've got a Google account ready to roll. And if you haven't had an account for any part of Google's world then a) goodness gracious me, that's impressive in this day and age, and b) the good news is that it's quick, easy and painless.

Don't be tempted to fob off the job of Google Analytics set-up to someone else, like an external web designer. If they use their own Google account to get things going, you could run into major issues down the road if you find yourself no longer working with them and unable to get ownership access of your own website's analytics. A scary thought — and one that should make the acquiring or use of your own Google account highly palatable!

Once you have an account, it's as simple as heading to https://www.google.com/analytics and following the instructions to fill in your website's details. It's also free, unless you're an absolutely massive company with multi-millions of hits per month — then you're looking at heading into the realm of Google Analytics 360, which demands a princely sum of at least US$150,000 a year. However, I would suspect that if you're playing in that world, you're probably leaving the SEO (and its reporting!) to your in-house experts.

IDENTIFYING THE STUFF THAT MATTERS

Google Analytics can provide data on all kinds of aspects of traffic and visitor behaviour. But the first place to check in on when your main interest is how your SEO changes are doing is organic search traffic.

In the 'Acquisition' section of the Google Analytics menu, there's an option under 'All Traffic' called 'Channels'. That section is where you'll see a breakdown of all the different kinds of ways people have found themselves on your website. There may be links from social media posts or email marketing, people may have typed your web address straight into their browser, or they may have clicked through from a PPC (pay per click) ad, if you've set those up. But we're interested (for the time being) in one particular area: organic search.

Clicking through to the organic search data will provide you with a whole lot of valuable information — whether for your own purposes or for reporting to your wider team. You'll be able to see overall numbers for different acquisition criteria (where your various website visitors are coming from) such as number of sessions, percentage of new sessions and number of new users; behaviour criteria like bounce rate, pages per session and average session duration; as well as a breakdown of all that information for different keywords.

ACQUISITION – SPEAKING IN SESSIONS

A session, in this context, refers to a user taking actions within your website in one sitting, within a specified timeframe. Those actions could be clicking from one page to another, filling in a form, scrolling down a page — basically just engaging with the website in some meaningful way. Google's default setting for a session is defined as lasting until there has been no user activity for half an hour.

As the name hopefully suggests, 'new sessions' refers to sessions from first-time visitors to your website. This data — as well as the sheer number of new users — can give you a good sense of what proportion of users are returning to your website. But do keep in mind that this breakdown of data is still related solely to organic search.

This means new sessions are people visiting for the first time after searching X keyword, and other sessions are people who are repeat visitors searching with X keyword (although their previous session may have been with any keyword search — as long as it led them to your website). This data isn't taking into account second/third/umpteenth users who have gone directly back to your website (i.e. by typing in your web address directly, rather than relying on Google results).

BASING IT ON BEHAVIOUR

Understanding acquisition is crucial when it comes to ascertaining whether your SEO techniques are working — and what within your approach is working particularly well or not so well. However, behaviour is also a highly valuable source of information. There's no point hooking people in to your website with amazing keywords if they don't do anything once they get there, and instead just navigate back to Google.

So, the behavioural metrics are a vital part of the equation — whether the news they bear is good or bad. The bounce rate refers to sessions where the visitor leaves your website after visiting only the one page they initially clicked through to. That's not to say that 'bounced' sessions are useless — a person could click through to an informative article, read it, get the answers they need and continue on their browsing for the day, with your business name tucked into their brain for the future. It tends to depend what the page you're analysing is set up for. That said, as far as getting a sense of people undertaking actions throughout your website, you'll want to see as low a bounce rate as possible.

Officially, Google doesn't use Google Analytics data in its algorithms that create the page rankings on the search engine. However, in this era of RankBrain — which you're hopefully feeling fairly confident about after chapter 10 — it seems inevitable that bounce rate does in fact have an impact. If your website has an 80 per cent bounce rate and your top competitor (who is also aiming to rank on the same terms as you) has a 60 per cent bounce rate, RankBrain is going to interpret that as them being more effective at answering your target customers' needs. And, in turn, that means that they'll get priority in the rankings. Make sense?

So look at your bounce rate, and if it's north of 50 per cent, think about why that could be. Are people coming to your site on the basis of one search term that doesn't actually align with the information you're providing? By looking at the bounce rate on a keyword-by-keyword basis, you can see which search terms are hitting the mark with your visitors, and which ones aren't. Figure out whether you need to be adjusting your wording — either to avoid visits from people who are looking for something that really isn't relevant to what you're offering, or to make it more clear on the page they're arriving on that you do in fact have what they're looking for!

Pages per session is an obvious relative of bounce rate. More is good — but not essential, depending on a) the size of your website, and b) the actions you want visitors to be taking. If all they need to do is get to your website, check out what your services are and fill out a contact form to make a booking, that's potentially three pages for a full customer journey. If you're an e-commerce retailer, on the other hand, and you want customers to buy multiple items, then more pages in a session will suggest that they are at the very least browsing multiple items. You'd obviously then need a different set of data to understand actual purchasing habits.

Similarly, average session duration is a metric that will depend on what your website is aiming to achieve. If the goal is simply for people to get in touch with you for more personalised information, a long session isn't necessarily a good thing — you might not be making that call to action clear enough, or you might be making the path to that basic action too complicated. But if you have a lot of important and useful content for people to read or experience, then a long session is totally appropriate. Think about your website's aims and how your ideal user would navigate things — and develop a sense of what you want your ideal session duration to be.

TIME AFTER TIME

Getting a sense of movement over time is important for several reasons — which is why Google puts an easy-to-understand graph right on top of all the breakdown of numbers and columns that I've just run through. If your number of sessions has doubled in the past month, and you've just adjusted your website according to your new SEO tactics, that's a brilliant sign.

But there's more to that data than just confirming that your SEO changes are doing their job. Take a look at where the peaks and troughs are, if there are any discernible patterns. Is it a regular cycle, with drops at certain times of the year — and, if so, is that related to other conditions that you're already aware of?

This kind of information can play into all kinds of decision-making. For example, perhaps you have a product that is very seasonal. However, people start searching for related terms a solid month ahead of your usual marketing push. Is it time to reconsider that approach, and reach out to people who are planning things sooner, rather than later?

NOT ALL TRAFFIC IS CREATED EQUAL

A hundred thousand unique sessions looks great on a spreadsheet — but it's meaningless if 90 per cent of those sessions aren't from genuine potential customers. You may have heard about problems with 'bot' accounts on social media networks like Twitter. Every now and then, Twitter will do a massive cull of bot accounts, and some people will see their follower count suddenly dip. Real popularity has a whole lot more to do with the calibre of the followers than the sheer number.

The most obvious indicator is conversion — which I explored in chapter 9 through the engagement lens. Make sure you're using Google Analytics to its full potential on this front, including examining differences in conversion rates between new visitors and returning visitors.

Maybe you run a barbershop, or another business that is very specific to a location. You can't cut people's hair over the internet! One major factor in establishing the quality of the traffic headed your way will be to check out the geographical location of people visiting your website. If you're based in Kilbirnie but your traffic is coming from Karachi, you've got a problem — people are unlikely to be making an international pilgrimage en masse for a haircut, no matter how amazing you are at your job! Geographical data is one of the many different permutations that you can investigate on Google Analytics — so have a look around and see what's going on.

Thinking back to the session-duration metric, that's another easy way of sorting the wheat from the chaff. If people are visiting your website and immediately clicking something, but wrapping up their visit within a few seconds, they probably aren't getting anything from your site — and you're not getting anything from them.

You can get a better sense of how people are engaging with your page using specialised tools such as Hotjar or Crazy Egg. These tools provide you with a 'heat map' of your web pages, allowing you to see exactly where people are clicking. You might think that your website is perfectly streamlined, but tools like these might let you see that people are struggling to figure out where to click to book, for example.

SORTING SEGMENTS

While some businesses are incredibly niche and only have one type of customer with one way of browsing the web, most will have a bit more breadth. And as far as metrics go, this is where segmentation can play an incredibly useful role. If you have an online bookshop, you might expect to have some visitors who are looking for a specific title, while others are looking for a user-friendly place to browse for a gift. Their browsing habits and objectives are going to look rather different from one another.

The visitor looking for a specific book might type the title into a search field, then perhaps try the author if that didn't work, and then abandon ship. Or they find it, let out a sigh of relief, and immediately purchase it. Either way, it's a quick session — the answer is ultimately yes or no and the ensuing actions are swift.

The visitor who isn't looking for anything in particular but instead looking for ideas will find a search field less useful than a clear and effective navigation system. You want to make sure that if they're looking for a pop psychology book for their dad, they can easily find their way to where the pop psychology books can be found.

CASE STUDY: DRILLING DOWN TO THE DETAIL AT EVENTFINDA

For event discovery platform and ticketing site Eventfinda, tracking key metrics and measuring the impact of search-marketing activity has always been important. The New Zealand site alone sees over 1.3 million visits a month, and almost 90 per cent of them come via organic search, so keeping an eye on its SEO is vital to its business model.

CEO James McGlinn has always ensured Eventfinda focuses on understanding audience segments, in order to deliver the best user experience. When an algorithm change caused a 25 per cent drop in traffic to the company's Australian site, the vital importance of SEO came to the fore.

'We knew that SEO wasn't just a tick in the box and that we needed to really understand our audiences and how they saw the site in order to make the user experience compelling for them. We were monitoring our analytics and constantly looking for indicators of success, but we soon realised that if we weren't crystal clear on our audiences and hadn't broken these segments down, we were effectively driving forward without looking under the hood,' McGlinn explains.

For Eventfinda, its two audience categories – those who want to access information about a specific event and those who more generally want to see what's on – signify very different objectives and on-site behaviour. It was clear that looking at high-level aggregate metrics like how many people were on the site, or how long visitors spent interacting with it, was not delivering a clear picture on its own. This is where segments came in.

McGlinn created custom dashboards that display next to each other and capture traffic, time on site and bounce rate (among other metrics) for visits via organic 'discovery' searches and organic 'detail' searches for a specific event. In this way, he was able to see how these different types of searches shifted compared to each other. McGlinn now checks the numbers daily – taking a long-range view to consider the day, and the week, in the context of a whole year. He makes sure the metrics remain front and centre for the team too, with big screens displaying charts on the walls of the office.

Of course, there are numbers and then there are the meaningful insights that come when you understand the numbers.

'The dashboard data enables us to see anomalies,' McGlinn explains. 'This signals that we need to investigate something further. From there we drill down to try to explain it.'

The first place they look is at their own activity, which is tracked and recorded as much as possible. All the iterative changes that McGlinn and his team make to the sites paint a picture; each time they tweak some part of either their on-page or off-page strategy, they add a tag in Google Analytics to signal this. When they then see a shift in engagement occur in the numbers, they can go back to look at those tags and get an idea of what's working, or what isn't. If nothing they have done seems to account for the shift, they look to algorithm changes, which can sometimes – although not always – explain the results. At the end of the day, though, its search engine is Google's proprietary software, and it doesn't always give everything away.

But back to the 25 per cent drop in traffic that I mentioned earlier in this story – what did the analytics say there? It took some time to uncover, and a lot of drilling down, but eventually McGlinn got to the point where he could see that it was just one type of traffic that had dipped, which was affecting the overall numbers. This discovery became the catalyst for ensuring this level of detail was constantly monitored.

The results of this approach speak for themselves. Not only has the Australian site regained the traffic that it dropped, the New Zealand site has continued to grow consistently.

'Despite changes in the competitive landscape, the internet itself and the way we are all interacting with it over the last thirteen or so years, I believe our relentless focus on our search metrics has been key to our success,' McGlinn says. Maintaining and growing an audience that size, and adding more than $100 million in ticket sales to its operations, would certainly indicate that something is working.

TRACKING YOUR OWN CHANGES

Just as you might utilise the 'track changes' functionality on a document that you're editing for a colleague, it's wise to track where and when you make changes to your website. A quick flag in Google Analytics that corresponds to when alterations take place can hugely streamline the process of understanding how things are working.

As well as looking at the sheer numbers and percentages that relate to visitors, Google Analytics provides other insights that can prove highly useful — from links to keywords to virtually everything else that has been mentioned in this book so far!

LOOKING AT LINKS

It's clear by now that links from other sources are a huge slice of the SEO pie — and Google Analytics allows you to see where the links to your website are coming from. This will also factor in to your assessment of the quality of your traffic — if you're getting a whole lot of links from a spammy domain, then there might be an issue with the calibre of visitors coming through. But if you've got some high-quality domains listed, you can feel more confident in that traffic.

It's also a chance to assess whether there are any major gaps. If you've been doing extensive guest blogging for another business website that you know gets great traffic but you're not seeing the links, maybe go and check it out for yourself. Have they included a link near the top of your article as well as at the bottom? Is it correct? Is it there at all?

DOMAIN AUTHORITY

Again, we've examined domain authority back in chapters 12 and 13 — but take it into account when setting up any reporting templates. It's not something that needs to be checked in on as regularly as other data, but it's still worth including to ensure that you're going up in the number stakes rather than down. Or, at the very least, staying firmly in one place!

KEYWORDS

Seems obvious, but worth mentioning. After you've gone to so much trouble developing, confirming and then integrating your keywords, you want to monitor how successful they are. Google Analytics can provide you with insight into what keywords are going gangbusters and which ones aren't perhaps as powerful as you thought. This doesn't mean going full slash and burn on your content — it just means re-examining the way that certain phrases and words are used if necessary.

SPEED DEMONS

The worst demons are speed demons — but, in SEO, the demons of speed are the ones that drag you down rather than rev you up. Pay attention to fluctuations in your pages' load speeds. We know by now that a slow load time equals a bad user experience, which equals a poor opinion of your page from Google's algorithm. If your load time suddenly increases, drill down to investigate what could be the cause of the problem. This is where flagging changes will really come in handy.

The potential of what you can measure on an ongoing basis is really as big as your imagination. Data gathering is a crucial part of the process of ensuring a constantly improving and developing website. There's no use attempting a 'set and forget' approach in this day and age — with algorithms and requirements constantly evolving, the only way to know for sure whether you're playing the game correctly is to check the stats. And if you're a really data-driven person, scoop up all that Google Analytics and other tools can throw at you — and interpret that information to create some awesome outcomes for you and your business.

CHAPTER SUMMARY

» Google Analytics is the free tool you need to kick-start your metric management.

» Take into account the nuances of your business and website before making assumptions on what counts as good or bad rates in your analytics.

» Get to know both acquisition and behavioural data to maximise your understanding of your customers.

» Remember the importance of tracking keywords and links as well as generating them.

SIXTEEN:

CRYSTAL BALL GAZING – THE FUTURE OF SEO

How many times have you wished you had a crystal ball? It would come in handy for predicting Lotto results, knowing which horse to back in the office Melbourne Cup pool, and even avoiding the unfortunate scenario of doubling up on dishes at a pot-luck dinner. It would also be fantastic in business.

While I can't tell you everything that the future will bring, I can tell you what I believe lies ahead from a search-marketing point of view. We've seen a hugely rapid rate of change in the last decade or two — from the first retail transaction over the web in 1994, to smartphones and camera phones, to social networking and the emergence of AI — and the years ahead are unlikely to be any different, with all manner of innovations changing the way we experience and interact with the world. We're now searching the internet on computers, tablets and phones as well as voice-activated assistants like Siri, Alexa, Amazon Echo and Google Home — and this is having an impact.

While some of the shifts might be subtle, and will likely feel like natural extensions of what we have now, others are set to be revolutionary. Let's take a look . . .

IN THE NEAR FUTURE . . .

As I emphasised at the start of this book, SEO is not a 'tick in the box' — it's not an activity to approach with a 'we've done it, cool, let's move on' attitude. Instead, SEO requires continuous, iterative improvements. Even once you achieve a high ranking for your chosen keyword (or words!), you have to keep putting in the work to stay there. This won't change.

In fact, some indications show that it will become even more difficult to 'win' at SEO. For starters, it's believed that while the total number of searches on Google keeps growing, the rate of this growth is plateauing. Not only that, click-through rates on organic searches are starting to decline — especially on mobile. This is a direct result of search engines evolving the way they serve up results. In Google's moves to display more rich results, they are becoming essentially an 'answer engine' as opposed to a list of search results on these devices.

Recent research by Jumpshot, which analyses tens of billions of Google searches in the US each month, found that click-through rates for organic search on desktop computers dropped from 71 per cent in November 2015 to 65 per cent in February 2018. Over the same period, organic search click-throughs on mobile devices have fallen from 66 per cent to 39 per cent. 'No click' search data adds to this picture, reinforcing the point I made at the end of the paragraph above. On mobile devices, no-click searches have risen from 33 per cent in November 2015 to 61 per cent in February 2018.

So why is this? Google is working hard to solve searchers' queries on the SERP (search engine results page), without mobile users needing to dive any further. The same does not apply to desktop; no-click searches there have only risen from 28 per cent to 34 per cent, and have remained relatively static for the last couple of years, pointing to the fact that desktop searchers still like to research and click around, as opposed to the quick answers we require when we are, perhaps, out and about.

Without a doubt, we'll continue to see changes across different platforms as the ways we interact with and use our devices change. However, these shifts are going to, frustratingly, mean that organisations and brands are influencing searchers without earning trackable clicks. While it may end up being harder to measure accountability metrics, this also points to the importance of creating rich results and investing in 'on the SERP SEO'.

'ON-THE-SERP' SEO: POSITION ZERO

Throughout this book, we've looked at all the things that will help your website to appear on the first page of Google search results for your chosen keywords. However, more and more businesses will also be wanting to optimise for the 'answer box' or 'featured snippet block' at the top of Google's search results page. This is what is referred to as 'position zero'.

Remember when we talked about long-tail keywords — all those instances when users type an entire question into their search bar? Position zero is where these types of searches come into their own. These answer boxes, which appear as the top organic result on SERPs, just after the ads, tend to include a summary of the answer, extracted from a web page, as well as a link to the page, the page title and its URL.

Although the prevalence of no-click results and Google answering queries on the SERP alone is increasing, this doesn't mean that your achievement of position zero will not result in any clicks; people do still click through from here. In fact, a Hubspot study of high-volume keywords revealed that when their content ranked for position zero, it produced a 114 per cent increase in click-throughs — even when that page already held the top organic ranking position.

On-the-SERP SEO certainly doesn't negate all your other SEO efforts either — in fact, Google selects the content for position zero based on the relevance of your content to the search query and the other SEO-ranking factors of your site. The snippet doesn't always come from the first-placed organic result either, but instead one of the first 10 organic results based on the question at hand.

More ways to optimise for position zero will come about but, in essence, as always your content needs to give people the most direct answers possible to their questions. Remember that search engines are, effectively, also businesses. I know I've mentioned this before, but their primary concern is delivering the best user experience which, in their case, means giving searchers the information they're looking for as quickly and efficiently as possible. To really understand the impact of position zero, it's useful to consider the other changes that will be driving our search behaviours.

IT'S VITAL TO CONSIDER VOICE SEARCH

No discussion of the future of SEO would be complete without exploring the impact of an increase in voice search.

At Pure SEO, we've been optimising for voice search for some time already, and it's my belief that it will continue to permeate everything we do (both in our roles here, as well as our lives as consumers).

According to Google, voice search already accounts for 20 per cent of all Google mobile search queries. Not only that, but 41 per cent of adults — and 55 per cent of teens — use voice search daily. Voice search has increased by 35 times in the last decade — and it's not just for mobile either. Twenty-five per cent of all Windows 10 desktop searches are done via voice. That's right: more and more of us are talking to our computers and smart speakers (like Amazon Echo) — not just to our phones. Some claim that it's a matter of time before smart speakers like this will become like refrigerators: every home will have one.

Either way, the (near) future implications for search are huge. Perhaps as a combination of its speed and convenience, it's predicted that by 2020, 50 per cent of all searches will be done by voice, and intermediary devices like keyboards will become a thing of the past.

So how is this going to affect SEO? It's probably not a huge surprise to you that searching with your voice is very different to searching with your fingers. For one, it's far more conversational, as we're using natural, human language — which will have an impact on both the content we expect to see and the on-page SEO and keyword research that businesses and brands are undertaking. (Remember right back to chapter 1, my emphasis on long-tail keywords that might represent the first thing that pops into a searcher's head, as opposed to the most succinct terminology? Here's further reason why!)

We're searching via different methods, too. As of early 2018, 58 per cent of US consumers had used voice search to find local business information in the last 12 months. Google also claims that queries that end with ' . . . near me now' have risen by 150 per cent over the last two years, signalling huge opportunities for local business search marketing, as we explored in chapter 7.

However, if you're still not sure whether dynamic or sensory search results (those that respond to both visual and voice search) are really that important, consider this: research by Slyce.it shows that 74 per cent of shoppers feel text-only search is insufficient for finding the products they want. Add to that, too, the fact that Gartner research predicts that in just a few short years — by 2021 — organisations that redesign their websites to support visual and voice search will increase e-commerce sales by up to 30 per cent.

It's time that brands and businesses start to think about how they want to sound, rather than just how they want to look. Voice search naturally opens up conversations — digital assistants and smart speakers will typically read the top answer that appears, so make sure some of your content is broken down into 20–30 seconds (roughly two or three sentences) of 'speakable structured data', which can easily be converted to audio content through 'text-to-speech' (TTS).

Not only do you need to think about the TTS usability of your content, but the concept of a 'brand voice' is set to take on a whole new (much more literal) meaning. It's unlikely to be long before our devices are relaying messages from brands, as opposed to just directly reading your text.

A VIEW TO VISUAL SEARCH

Although it's not getting quite so much publicity, visual search is changing the way we interact with our environment, too. Although we've long had the ability to add alt tags to images so they are more likely to show up on the Google SERP (images are returned for 26.8 per cent of search queries on Google), we're beginning to see cameras operate as a visual discovery tool; take image recognition apps Google Lens and Pinterest Lens as an example.

These allow you to point your phone's camera at something and then ask for an answer to a specific question, or to see things that are related or similar. For example, you might be out on your morning walk. You see a stunning flower in one of your neighbours' gardens, so you use Google Lens to snap a picture and find out what it is so you can plant some yourself. You can also use the app to recognise restaurants or cafés so you can easily see a pop-up of reviews, opening hours, etc.

Pinterest Lens works similarly; when you're out in the world and spot something interesting, you can snap a picture and then discover related ideas. For example, if you have an ingredient you want to use up, you can take a picture of it and discover recipes that use that item. Or if you're not sure what to wear with your new brown shoes, just take a picture and scroll through the different outfit-inspiration and styling ideas.

The adoption of image search, as opposed to text, is huge. More than 600 million visual searches are performed each month on Pinterest alone! Not only that, but visual search is the building block for AR (augmented reality) and VR (virtual reality), both of which use AI to identify items and then overlay digital elements with knowledge of the real world. This is a game-changer for search, social and content marketing. The wide adoption of visual search means the likelihood of AR at least being adopted by the mainstream is much higher.

So how do you make sure your site is best optimised for all of those who are operating in this 'point, shoot, search' mode? Product searches via this method will likely be loaded with more buying intent than your more traditional 'browsing' or market-research engagement. To make the most of this, brands and businesses need to make sure that all of the information about their products and services is clear, from a visual point of view. Make sure your branding is consistent and your logo is displayed. However, this doesn't apply only to products. A restaurant, for example, is going to want to make sure its outside branding is visible from the street view.

Pay attention, too, to your metadata as it relates to the visual elements of your site. As we've explored in the earlier chapters, it will be vital to have the best possible information in alt tags, captions and anchor text. Other best-practice SEO strategies apply to visual search also, as does good marketing and branding. Image-based platforms, like Pinterest and Instagram, are already upping the game in terms of the standard of visual information that we expect to see, so make sure that the images you use to represent your brand or business are attractive and professional.

Sensory search represents, in my opinion, one of the foremost opportunities in digital marketing in the coming years. We're beyond the 'keyboard and mouse' era, with visual and voice-based computing via our smartphones and other devices. Visual and voice search will enable marketers to engage more meaningfully with their audience at any stage of the purchase journey. Static websites will become a thing of the past as we see more and more brands embrace interactive experiences that can be accessed anywhere, any time and from any device.

HOW THINGS MIGHT CHANGE WITH THE INTERNET OF THINGS (IOT)

Speaking of anywhere, anytime and from any device, forward-thinking brands and businesses are already starting to factor in the impact that the proliferation of the 'Internet of Things' (IoT) will have on search results. What do we mean by Internet of Things? At a basic level, IoT refers to the interconnection (via the internet) of devices embedded in everyday objects that are able to send and receive data.

It's the internet's move into the physical world, and almost every industry is embracing it — from manufacturing and agriculture to transportation, not to mention consumer uses in wearable devices (such as watches and fitness trackers) and gadgets in our homes. Vehicles, appliances, buildings, factories, equipment and machinery are all being embedded with electronics, software, sensors and connectivity. The global market for IoT is projected to reach US\$7.1 trillion, with 30 billion IoT devices, by 2020.

An area that will touch all of us as consumers is that of smart-home technology, and it won't just be the domain of luxury gimmicks for wealthy homeowners. We're already seeing thermostats through to door locks that are WiFi enabled. In the last few years, though, we've seen all sorts of gadgets released as individual smart components; we've not yet seen a singular technology to get them all working together. I have no doubt that this is coming, and we will see everything become integrated with search.

Search ranking and visibility will still matter, but instead of a moment in time when searchers will turn their attention to directly engage with a search engine, queries will be more specific and contextual. Desktop and mobile interactions will no longer be the only domains search marketers need to be thinking about. Content will still need to be relevant to a query, but its relevance will also be combined with its usefulness *in that moment*.

Further extending on the importance of voice search, we're going to be talking to products in our homes — without the need for manual buttons, screens or interfaces — and they'll be answering us. They will be giving one answer, as opposed to a range that we can choose to click on, too, so that top-ranked spot is going to be even more important. And again, the points about long-tail keywords and conversational tone come into play here in the way we'll interact with these devices. The shift from purely keyword-based content to intention-based writing will amplify as we see the IoT take off.

I can imagine that search personalisation will also get all the more refined, as our 'things' connect to more and more of our environment and personal devices, and gather huge amounts of data about us, our personal lives and our preferences. It won't be long before we're seeing recommendations for products and services, or information pages served up before we even know we need them! We're also going to be interacting with information differently — as opposed to scrolling through websites and clicking around, we'll be following the most direct route to order more paper towels or find out how long it takes to bake a chicken.

AND FURTHER AFIELD STAR GAZING . . .

If talking to our appliances (and having them answer us!) feels a little too much like a scene out of the Jetsons, there's even more coming that will blow your mind. While our cars are not likely to start flying (just yet), it may not be long until they're driving without us.

Already we've got vehicles that actively assist us in navigating our way into even the tightest of car parks or, in some cases, park themselves without our input. And all the big guys are getting in on it. But whether you think driverless cars are going to be just a passing tech fad or the future of transportation, autonomous car technology is becoming more and more prevalent.

Why am I mentioning this here? It's just another example of the ways our search behaviours will continue to evolve and intersect with the rest of our lives.

Imagine you do a voice search on Google at home — for something you need to buy, something you want to do, or just the best place to get Thai food nearby. You get the results you are looking for — quickly and easily because Google has so well-optimised to ensure your best user experience — and decide to head out to purchase/do the thing in your driverless car. The technology in the car is WAYMO (self-driving car technology), so it knows what you have just searched for and starts to play something on the radio that is related. As you peer out the window, taking in the surroundings, the digital billboard you are looking at has changed; it is now also seamlessly showing you something related to the aforementioned search. This might sound spooky, but this is the level of personalisation that could be coming as a result of all the data that exists about you — and it all stems from search.

THE LAST WORD: SEO'S NOT GOING AWAY

It may be getting harder to 'win' when it comes to traditional SEO, but this does not mean that investment in SEO will be going away anytime soon. On the whole, interest in SEO is still massively higher than in other forms of web marketing, and that's unlikely to shift significantly in the foreseeable future.

As a field, search marketing is far more trustworthy than even a few years ago, as it's shed more of its ethically questionable 'black hat' reputation. However, this also means that there is greater competition vying for fewer traffic opportunities — perhaps because SEO is finally getting the investment it deserves from major brands and companies.

There are going to be great opportunities for those who are watching out for the trends that are coming, and we're excited to be poised at the forefront of what is happening in search marketing in our corner of the world. Not only will we continue looking at how things evolve here in our own backyard, we'll also be keeping an eye on what those in more mature markets are doing.

For a final word, I reached out to Rand Fishkin, the so-called 'Godfather of SEO' (otherwise known as 'The Wizard of Moz'). His thoughts mirror some of my own impressions and many of the myths I dispelled at the start of this book:

» SEO has had a long history as a field where relatively few organisations invested seriously because of a perception of shady behaviour and tactics. It's also been a field where the dominant players (Google and Yahoo! and Microsoft in the early days, now mostly just Google) were happy to provide a tremendous amount of traffic and value without taking much for themselves (besides a small percent of clicks to their sponsored results). In my opinion, both those trends are reversing now and will continue to. That's going to have a huge impact on how practitioners and strategic investors think about organic search.

» To start, SEO is finally a big, serious investment that almost every web marketing team makes. That increased competition at a time when search growth is plateauing creates more players vying for the same traffic, which means it's harder and harder to stand out. Every month you don't invest in SEO is a month when your competitors will, and eventually, even if you have a long head-start, they'll catch up and surpass you.

» SEO, like any marketing tactic, isn't fire and forget. It requires ongoing, consistent improvement just to keep pace with the market. Unfortunately, many people and organisations still think that once they achieve rankings or traffic, they no longer need to continue making those investments. As a result, there's constant turnover in even the most lucrative search results.

» Those who want to win in SEO long term will have to follow in the footsteps of the few organisations who've done it right – made SEO a core competency, built a dedicated team and leveraged consultants to help them advance.

» The second piece of SEO's future is about how Google and searchers are changing the landscape of the industry.

Google's taking more and more of the 'answers' to search queries for themselves by providing rich data (often scraped from your websites) right in the search results. They're advancing voice answers, which provide no search traffic or analytics to those who serve the queries. And they're creating new sectors of their business that directly compete in certain sectors against the existing players (like Google Flights, Google weather results, Google Maps and local pages, etc).

» The endgame of this is fewer available clicks going to organic results and more queries answered by Google itself, benefiting Google, but not the websites or businesses providing the information. That's a bitter pill to swallow, but it means those in the SEO field will need to think more about how Google is presenting their information, and what investments might need to be made in 'on-SERP' SEO and voice answer results.

» We're living through a maturing industry, with a global monopoly leveraging its power to take opportunity away from other players in favour of benefiting itself and its shareholders. Those who accept that reality and invest in tactics to seek out new opportunities will survive and thrive, while others will find SEO to be a more challenging, less generous marketing investment.

Well done on getting to the end of this book and taking steps to get to the top of Google search. Whilst there is a lot of work to achieving good search engine rankings, you can now see that it is very achievable with a bit of planning and hard work. See you at the top of the search rankings!

INDEX